THE GOONS
THE STORY

ACKNOWLEDGEMENTS

I would like to thank Dorothy (Dot) Grafton and Mrs Rita Browell for their help and the loan of their prized photographs and I would particularly like to thank John Fisher for all his kindness to me, not just over this book, but for all the years.
Norma Farnes

It would have been impossible for me to have contributed to this book were it not for the opportunity to refer to several previously published Goon Show texts. The painstaking work of Roger Wilmut and Jimmy Grafton in The Goon Show Companion makes it an invaluable record of the show. I am also indebted to David Nathan for his The Laughtermakers and to Alfred Draper for The Story Of The Goons.

I have also drawn on research and interviews conducted for The Goon Show Preservation Society which has unearthed stories, particularly from Peter Eton and John Browell, never told before.
Chris Smith

Pictures courtesy of John P Hamilton, George W Brown, Adrian Rigelsford, Hulton Getty, PA News Library.

First published in 1997 by
Virgin Publishing Ltd
332 Ladbroke Grove
London
W10 5AH

A catalogue record for this book is available from the British Library

ISBN 1-85227-679-7

Designed by Design 23, London
Printed by Hillman Printers, Frome

THE GOONS
THE STORY

Edited by Norma Farnes

Virgin

CONTENTS

Introduction

When Rod Green of Virgin Publishing first came to me with the idea of producing The Goons – A Celebration, I thought it was a good one. Virgin has published a number of successful illustrated books in their Celebration series, including one with Spike which I liked very much. Several meetings later, when we were discussing the content of the book, I said, 'Everyone has their own stories about the Goons, how they started, the dramas, the ups and downs, the tantrums, but I think that the only person now who really knows what went on is Spike. Someone should interview him along with Harry and Eric.' Why did I say that? I should have realised I was setting myself up because Rod, who gets away with murder with me, immediately said, 'Of course, and you should do the interviews. Who else? You know them best.'

Several meetings later Rod decided that I should write an introduction. Why did I agree? Although I've been surrounded for the last thirty years by some formidable talent I'm certainly not a writer myself. As I became aware of the shape that the book was taking, however, I realised that I wanted this to be the definitive Goon Show book. Rod agreed that we should take it out of the Celebration series, Spike suggested the simple title The Goons – The Story, and here it is.

When I knew I had to write this introduction, I started looking through some of my memorabilia for inspiration and found a very early Goon Show Classics LP signed by Spike and Harry and with a dedication from John Browell. It says 'My love – and undying thanks for smoothing my passage, John Browell XXX'. What on earth was that all about? I've never really collected

Spike with John Browell during a break in Goon Show recording.

John Browell.

autographs like that, so I've no idea why it had been signed in this way. The LP included The Histories Of Pliny The Elder and The Dreaded Batter Pudding Hurler Of Bexhill-on-Sea. John didn't produce either of these. Pliny, in fact, was produced by Pat Dixon, one of the very few shows that Pat produced himself. Had this been The Last Goon Show Of All LP, I could have understood the dedication as John and I worked together on that show. The signed LP cover was, and still is, a mystery to me but it did bring back fond memories of John Browell.

John rang me in October 1971 to say that the BBC wanted to do a special Goon Show to celebrate 50 years of the BBC and asked if Spike would write the script. Spike didn't want to do it, but I thought it was such a good idea – I must stop entertaining these good ideas – and over a period of three weeks I eventually persuaded Spike to write the script for The Last Goon Show Of All. With that established, John said, 'Let's see when they're all available.' This, I knew, was <u>not</u> a good idea. I knew that Pete would say, 'I'll do it if Spike will, any time he's available.' Spike would say, 'I'll do it when Harry is available,' and Harry would say, 'I'll do it when Spike is available.' As I said to John, it will take a year, the three of them will have us running

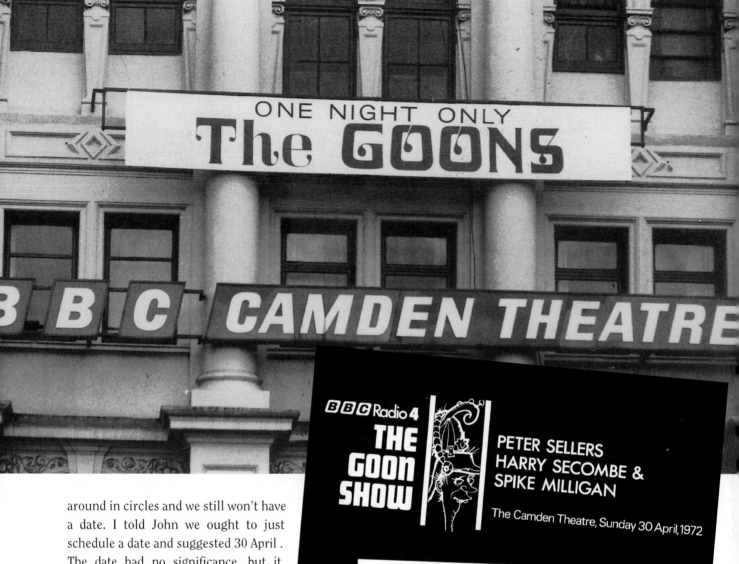

ONE NIGHT ONLY
The GOONS

BBC CAMDEN THEATRE

BBC Radio 4
THE GOON SHOW

PETER SELLERS
HARRY SECOMBE &
SPIKE MILLIGAN

The Camden Theatre, Sunday 30 April, 1972

BBC Radio 4 presents
THE GOON SHOW

Specially written for the 50th Anniversary of the British Broadcasting Corporation by SPIKE MILLIGAN
Produced by JOHN BROWELL

Dramatis Personae

Hercules Grytpype-Thynne	A plausible public school villain and cad	
Mate	Drains cleared while you wait	
Bluebottle	A cardboard cut-out liquorice and string hero	PETER SELLERS
Major Denis Bloodnok	A military idiot, coward and bar	
Henry Crun	A thin ancient, and inventor	
HARRY SECOMBE	Ned of Wales / Neddy Seagoon / The Houses of Parliament	True blue British idiot and hero always
Eccles	The original Goon	
Count Moriarty	A French scrag and lackey to Grytpype-Thynne	SPIKE MILLIGAN
Minnie Bannister	Spinster of the Parish and inseparable from Henry	
Ellinga	Batman to Bloodnok, singer and what-have-you	RAY ELLINGTON
The Conks	Dutch nose swinger and harmonica player extraordinaire	MAX GELDRAY

Orchestra conducted by PETER KNIGHT

Assistant to Producer Martin Fisher. Production Secretary Anne Ling. Sound Team Eric Young, Maggie Dean, Mardi Eyles, Michael Cowles.
Original members of the Wally Stott Orchestra – Trumpets Alan Franks, Freddy Clayton, Basil Jones, Stan Roderick, Tommy McQuater.
Trombones George Chisholm, Lad Busby, Jack Armstrong, Don Lusher. Saxes Bob Burns, Frank Reedy, Harry Smith, E. O. Pogson,
Bill Povey, Ken Dryden. Harp Osian Ellis, David Snell. Percussion Jock Cummings.
The Ray Ellington Quartet Dick Katz, Judd Proctor, Ian White, Bill Eyden.

around in circles and we still won't have a date. I told John we ought to just schedule a date and suggested 30 April. The date had no significance, but it would help to get them motivated. Miracle of miracles, that ended up as the date the show was actually recorded!

Spike wrote the script, they all turned up, Harry brought the brandy, Peter did not have laryngitis and Spike remembered the date. Maybe I should explain the laryngitis reference. While I was browsing through my memorabilia, I came across a note about one of the Goon Shows which made me realise what dramas John Browell must have gone through. Who Is Pink Oboe? was recorded way back on 12 January, 1959 and the note said, 'Peter had throat trouble' and at the eleventh hour John had to replace him with Kenneth Connor, Valentine Dyall and a few others. I wondered if Pete really did have throat trouble, or whether this was the birth of his famous 'laryngitis' excuse. Pete, you see, could do the most marvellous impersonation of someone with laryngitis that I have ever heard and consequently, when he didn't want to do a film, or a gig, or go anywhere, he would phone using his 'laryngitis' voice and say, 'Er . . . sorry, I've got laryngitis.' As you would expect, he was very convincing. Alternatively, he would just do his disappearing act and leave someone else to impart the bad news.

Although I had not been involved in the original Goon Show series, I have heard all of the stories from Pete, Spike and Harry. They often spoke about the heroic war record of Jimmy Grafton, who was such an inspiration to them in the beginning. This avuncular man had been involved in bitter hand-to-hand fighting at Arnhem. When his position was being overrun by enemy tanks, he used his radio to order a vicious British artillery barrage to bombard his own map reference! Having learnt of this, I can well understand the deep respect Spike, Harry and Peter felt for Jimmy Grafton.

Then there was the story of the infamous monkey, Johnny, at the Grafton Arms. Spike remembers eventually becoming friends with it after finding it a rug and a nice warm place on top of a water tank, but I always wondered where the monkey had come from. I was convinced that there must be an exotic story about how Jimmy had acquired Johnny. No one I spoke to, however, could shed any light on the matter. Everyone just seemed to accept that Jimmy had a monkey. It was Jimmy's widow, Dot, who finally told me the true story. Dot said that a customer had come into the bar one day at the Grafton Arms and asked Jimmy if he wanted to buy a monkey. Jimmy thought it would make a lovely

present for Dot and the deal was done. It's not quite the exotic story I was looking for, but at least it solves the mystery.

This book is not, however, solely concerned with stories from the past. John Fisher's recent television programme Heroes of Comedy – The Goons was, as far as I am concerned, a wonderful show. Everyone interviewed for the programme was so complimentary about Spike. Jonathan Miller's observations that Spike 'was a major monument in British culture and had a tremendous sense of conceptual humour' and 'his work had the same importance as Alice In Wonderland [a great favourite of Spike's] and the Pickwick Papers' were tremendous tributes. Dick Lester said, 'He [Spike] has a thin skin surrealism which is very rare' and 'had the finest comedy mind in terms of extraordinary originality.' Dick mentioned that he had worked with some of the all-time greats, including Buster Keaton, and when I reminded him that Dick had compared him to Keaton, Spike said, 'Yes, I suppose mine were ideas, his were

share glo[...]
[A]rnhem men
[M]AJOR CALLED ON GUNS
[T]O SHELL OW[N]

[TO]DAY is told for the firs[t]
story of the relief of th[e]
[infa]ntry of the 43rd (Wess[ex]
It is a story that matches
[tro]ops against overwhelming [odds]
[res]cue effort of 250 men of the
[the]ir own supply line cut be[hind]
[th]rough enemy-held fenland
[tr]ucks" with precious cargoes
[af]ter; of a colonel who wa[s]
[th]em with the bayonet."
And of a major who deli[vered]
[ar]tillery barrage down on his

THE LA[ST]

The fight by the Dorsets
[b]ank of the River Lek. The
[...]men of the 250 brave rescue[rs]
The grim fight to reach
River Lek began on Septem[ber]
airborne landings.
That day, with the fe[rry]
[unpas]sable to armoured columns
make its first attempt t[o]
garrison.
Two brigades of infa[ntry]
crossed the Nijmegen br[idge]
Supported by a small numbe[r of]
tanks they had orders to b[reak]
through the dyke country, and [up]
up the Arnhem road, and t[o]
contact with the Airborne
still believed to be holding
Arnhem itself.

Relief essential

Very bitter fighting dev[eloped]
along the dyke roads and [in]
villages and woods of this [un-]
[ha]pitable fenland between [the]
[...] rivers. The drive up th[e]
road made no progress. [The]
tanks were encountered an[d a]
[vil]lage completely shattered
[...] fighting on the left of the [...]
Reports coming in durin[g]
showed that the Airborn[e were]
[still] holding out west of Arn[hem]
[...] already so tight and smal[l ...]
[...] R.A.F. in spite of galla[nt ...]
[...] had succeeded in droppin[g ...]
[...] per cent. of its paracht[...]
[...] inside the perimeter.
The Airborne were sh[ort of]
[am]munition, were likely to [...]
[...] food, and needed medic[al ...]
[...] relief had to be got to [them ...]
[...]out delay.

Crashed thro[ugh]

[C]olumns, [c]arrying an arm[oured]
battalion of the 43rd, a[nd]
a squadron of an ar[moured]
[divi]sion and reach "the [...]
[posi]tion and reach "the [...]
several "ducks" lo[aded with]
ammunition and food, [with men]
[in]fantry riding on the tanks
[and] carriers.
On the way five G[erman tanks]
broke into the column [...]
at a point where it [...]
split two-thirds of th[...]
With Tiger tanks [...]
up, the head of the co[lumn]
covering the ten per[...]
20 minutes, and rea[ched the ...]
bank.
Behind it, a compa[ny ...]
—Major H. Parker [...]
near Birmingham—[...]
gether a fighting for[...]
Piats he could mu[ster ...]
traps for the Tiger[...]
roads.

Tigers smashed

A German dispatch rider, leading
the hurrying tanks, was blown sky
high. Firing from the ditches on
the roadside, the Piat crews riddled
the first tank at 5-10 yards range
as it and a second tank behind
opened fire and endeavoured to
hide themselves in a smoke screen.
The first tank was set on fire, the
second ran into the ditch after
being hit. Two others following
up behind also ditched themselves
in their efforts to get off the road.
All four were brand new Tigers
which had passed out of the
Nuremberg factory only a fortnight
earlier.
The daring drive straight through
the German territory had
gained its end. But the effort
was to be in vain. As the men
struggled to get the laden "ducks"
down to the river in the darkness
each "duck" in turn slithered off
the narrow road into the dyke. No
supplies reached the Airborne that
[day].
The next day's attempt was
bigger, organised, armed with sup-
[...]made. A brigade, assault boats instead of
[...]plies and moved into [...]

COVERED WITHDRAWAL AT ARNHEM

Westminster Major's Party First To Link With Airborne Troops

MEN OF THE DORSETS DO OR DIE ATTEMPT

When it became evident to the military commanders at Arnhem that our gallant airborne forces would have to be withdrawn, two hundred and fifty men of the Dorset Regiment were entrusted with the task of contacting them and later covering their withdrawal.

Against overwhelming odds they battled on to the airborne men and some of the war's bitterest fighting was fought. The Germans went all out to frustrate our relief troops, for if they did the annihilation of the airborne men was certain.

FIGHT NOT IN VAIN

But the Dorset Regt. had no intention of wavering and giving ground. At the spearhead of their Force[s ...] party led by Major J. D. Grafton, of Gayfere street, Westminster [was] the first to make its objective —the link up with an airborne headquar[te]rs on the right.

Pushing inland, the Westminster officer and his men [gai]ned that precious elbow [ro]om to allow for the withdrawal of the Airborne troops. [It] was very costly fighting, but [Ma]jor Grafton knew that his [sol]diers' great and heroic [str]uggle had not been in vain, [...] nearly three thousand of [the] Airborne were safely evacu[ate]d.

[Th]ere is universal admira[tion] for men like Major [Gra]fton, who have gained not [onl]y the respect of the soldiers [of th]e Allied Armies, but the [ene]my himself, who acknow[ledg]ed that "the British fought [like] lions."

just tricks, mind you, brilliant tricks.'

Spike's peers heaped on the praise. After I had seen a rough cut of the show and talked to Spike about it, telling him all the wonderful things which had been said, I thought he would be delighted. All he said was, 'All this adulation and the BBC won't even repeat The Goon Shows on radio.' That is something he feels particularly passionate about and, of course, he's right. The Goon Shows should be repeated. The BBC have sold over 684,000 Goon Show cassettes and CDs . . . and they're still selling. Surely this proves the immense popularity and durability of the show. I have pressed the BBC many times to broadcast a series of repeats, so far to no avail. The warmth of affection and the respect for Spike demonstrated by those on the Heroes of Comedy show was, however,

Major James Grafton.

a tremendous tribute.

The first Goon Show was recorded on 28 May, 1951, and the last one on 28 January, 1960. I have often wondered why, at the peak of its popularity, Spike decided not to write any more Goon Shows. He told me, 'It would have been nice to have taken the money, but I didn't want to do what most shows have done and run the show until it had lost its energy and died – unfunny and unwanted.' I asked whether he had felt sad when he took that decision and what he did after the recording of the last show. He told me that Pete and Harry and he had gone out to dinner at a Czech restaurant in the Edgware Road. It was called Garblundens. Spike believes it was a German restaurant, but for some reason it was always known as the Czech restaurant. I had visions of the three

of them being morose and downhearted, but nothing could be further from the truth. It was business as usual. According to Spike, they had used what they thought was a very funny joke at that evening's recording, but it had not raised a laugh from the audience. The three of them spent the last night of The Goon Shows discussing the Deaf Gorilla Joke.

The joke, in case there's someone out there who hasn't heard it (never!!!) and who may be driven mad trying to figure out what it might be, goes as follows:

A man is sitting in the middle of a jungle clearing playing Brahms on his violin. His playing is exquisite and all the animals have gathered round to listen to this beautiful music. Suddenly, a gorilla comes out of the jungle, goes up to the man, grabs the violin and smashes it to the ground, wham–bam–bam! The animals look on in horror and the tiger says to the gorilla, 'What did you do that for?' and the gorilla says, 'Eh?' So, folks, that is how they celebrated the last night's recording of The Goon Show.

Spike's reflection on that time: 'Those years in that show just seem like a hectic dream . . . it was.'

Different people, of course, remember things in very different ways. The differences are even more pronounced when you are dealing with people with such fertile imaginations as, for example, Spike and Eric. Some of the statements in this book, therefore, differ slightly. But that's the way they remember things. For me, I just remember that Spike is Eccles, and always will be. One of my favourite quotes about him was written by writer and broadcaster Gary Bushell who, after one of Spike's TV appearances, wrote, 'I wish someone would do a deal with God and let Spike Milligan live forever.' Spike's response to that was, 'I wouldn't stop him.'

I would like the last words of this introduction to go to my dear friend John Browell. In 1974, John wrote this about the Goons, referring to Pat Dixon:

' . . . without whose behind the scenes pressure and connivance the BBC would never have been tricked into giving birth to the Goons. Wouldn't we – and they – have all been the poorer.'

Norma Farnes

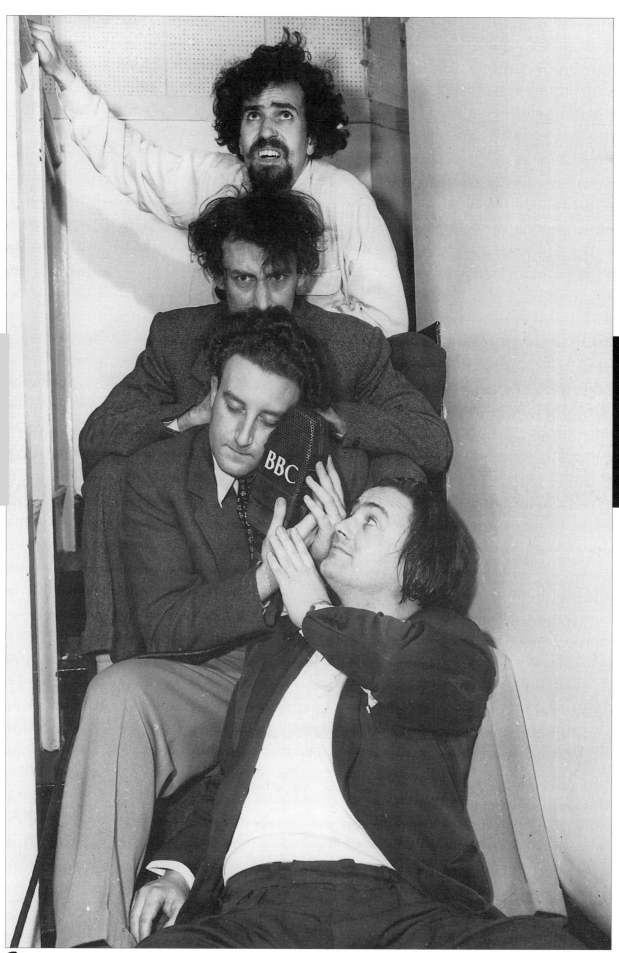

THE GOONS – The Story part 1

The Second World War proved to be a fertile setting for many of Spike Milligan's flights of fancy in what would become The Goon Show, although his war memoirs detail the terrible price he paid during that conflict to gain such inspiration. He frequently alluded to the war in subsequent interviews:

'I got used to seeing men jumping out of little holes and looking about with binoculars. Men looking out of tanks with binoculars. Always men looking out and throwing things at one another. I thought to myself, "This is mad."

Each of the Goons – Spike, Harry, Peter Sellers and Michael Bentine - had some experience of the War which left them more or less suspicious or sceptical about authority and its competence. They had each seen how things could work out on the ground, after all. Peter's escapades in the Air Force (he never flew) were more along the lines of cocking a snook at authority through his insubordinate impersonations of senior officers, which he and other close friends like David Lodge fondly recounted or wrote about in the years that followed.

Michael was more involved in aspects of reconnaissance or military intelligence and was somewhat reluctant to talk too freely about his army career (except its hilarious bumbling moments), yet he also developed that skewed perception of events and personalities that was so crucial in creating The Goon Show.

There's nothing like escaping from a war alive for building a

Michael Bentine, Spike Milligan, Peter Sellers and Harry Secombe – the Goons.

... than ever.

There seems to be more than a little promise in the plans of members of the "Goon's Club" —the story of which was first broken by Bill Boorne of the London *Evening News* last Saturday. Founder members of the Goon's are four ex-Windmill Theatre comedians and impressionists, namely Michael Bentine (now at the London Hippodrome), Alfred Marks (currently Grand, Brighton), Harry Secombe, and Peter Sellers (now at the London Palladium for two weeks). Also interested are scripter Spike Milligan and Jean Carson, who will be the first Goonness. Club badge is to be a humanised peanut— ambition of the group, to form themselves into a new style crazy gang after they have established themselves firmly as singles.

GOON'S CLUB.

Top: Michael Bentine served in military intelligence during the war.

Right: A relaxed Spike Milligan.

sense of optimism. Things can only get better, even if one's only major asset (apart from general health and a demob suit) is a talent to amuse or entertain. With the end of hostilities and a return to civilian life, it was clear that the futures of Peter, Spike, Harry and Michael would be in some form of entertainment career. As Spike said, 'It seemed silly to go on being serious after five very serious years. I suppose the idea was to get as far away as possible from what was normal. It was a reaction against the stringencies of war.'

They were far from being the only ones to draw this conclusion. Many of the names now familiar in British households as comedians or entertainers took their chances in show business as a result of wartime experiences in the Central Pool of Artistes, successfully keeping up troop morale. Spike's first engagements came as a musician, on trumpet or (as part of the Bill Hall Trio) playing guitar. '[After the Bill Hall Trio] I didn't work at all, just sort of wandered around. I'd meet Harry, and then I'd meet Peter Sellers, who was at the Windmill Theatre. They were successful. Somehow or other I ended up at Jimmy Grafton's pub in Victoria and I used to tell jokes. Harry was there – I'd play the piano and Harry would sing. Peter would come in and do a few impressions; Michael Bentine was there. We all used to laugh a lot. We had a strange sense of humour. Jimmy was writing for Derek Roy and asked me if I would like to write for him . . ."

Optimism, however, requires feeding in one fashion or another. With so many hopefuls seeking to break into show business it was not always easy to find the breaks. One crucial support to artistes in these years following 'demob' was the Grafton Arms, where the proprietor Jimmy Grafton was sympathetic to struggling young talent to the extent

The Goons raise a toast to future success.

of providing liquid (and literal) sustenance.

Grafton's, therefore, rapidly became the place where first introductions between a couple of the Goons led to firm friendships and the discovery of a shared lunatic sense of humour. Michael had become acquainted with Harry since they both performed comic turns at the Windmill Theatre, 'notorious' for its tableaux of motionless posed nudes. In between these tableaux, young comics took their chances, attempting to prise laughs out of an audience which had no real interest in listening to a comedian. They were there for the girls.

Harry's antics with a shaving mug, depicting how men of different ages shaved, and Michael's inspired use of the broken back of a chair as a variety of objects, made it obvious to both men that they shared the same quirky sense of humour. It was inevitable that Michael, who already knew of Graftons, would take Harry there, and this led to the meetings with Peter and Spike.

Peter's uncanny talents with mimicry eventually brought him work as an impressionist. Strange as it seems now, things happened slowly for him until, in desperation, he assumed the voices of both Kenneth Horne and Dickie Murdoch to gain access by telephone to senior producer Roy Speer at the BBC. Speer produced a Variety programme called Showtime. The ruse worked: 'Kenneth Horne' was put through to Roy Speer, and recommended to an appreciative Speer that he employ a fantastic new talent called Peter Sellers. Then Sellers had to take the plunge.

Peter: It's me . . . Peter Sellers.
Speer: Eh? What's that?

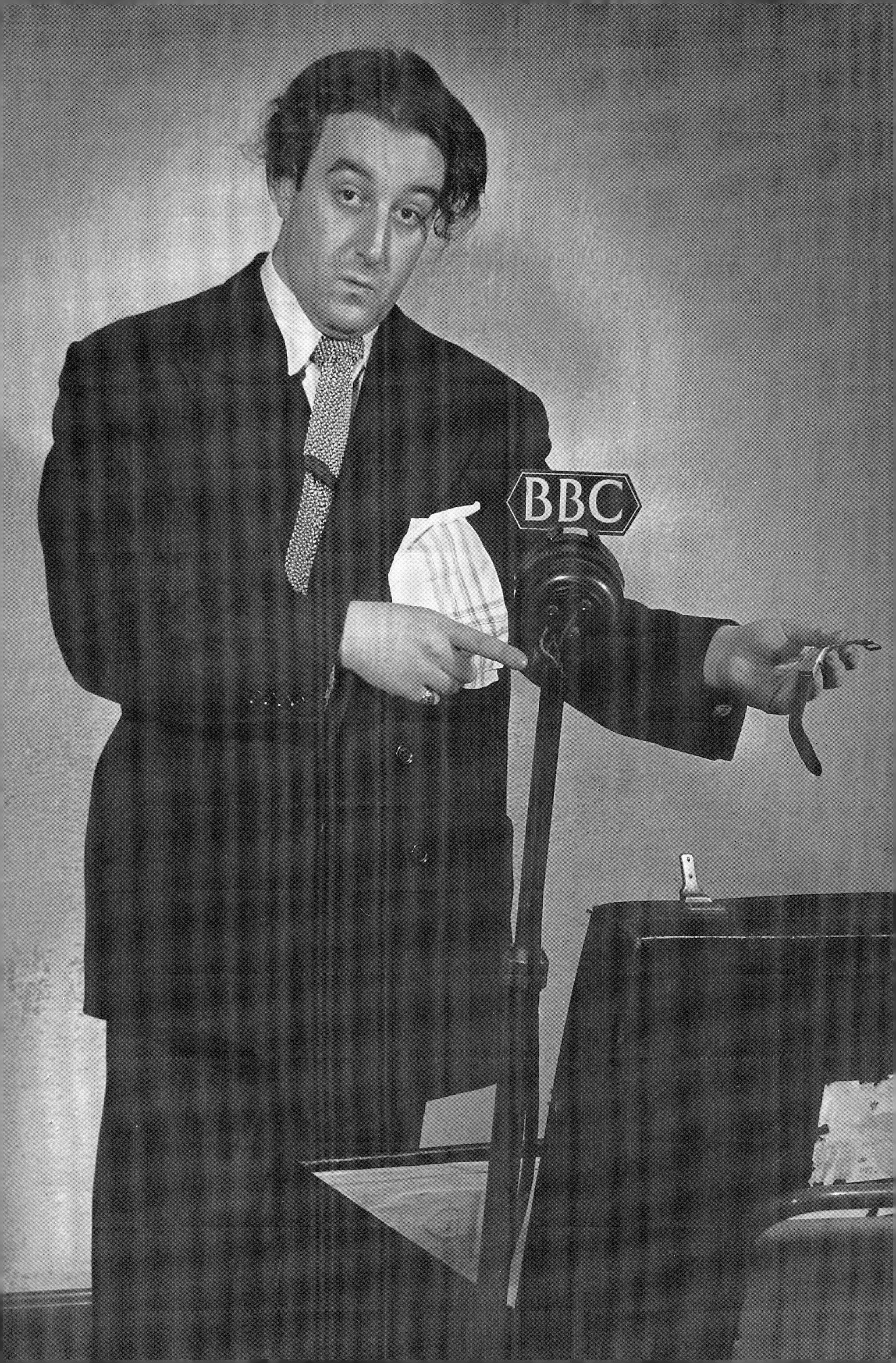
BBC

Peter: It's me, Peter Sellers . . . This was the only way I could reach you . . .
and could I have a spot on your programme?
(pause. Then, said with deliberation)
Speer: You . . . cheeky . . . young . . . sod! What do you do?
Peter: Well, obviously I do impressions!

Opposite: Peter Sellers' talent
for impressions led to his first
radio work.

Peter successfully auditioned for Showtime and became the first of the
Goons to be established as a performer on BBC radio. This was a crucial strategic
entrée for future efforts to get The Goon Show on air.

Spike had a slightly different introduction
to working in the BBC, as a contributing
gag writer, via Jimmy Grafton,
for the late-1940s radio show Hip Hip Hoo
Roy (John Browell, who later became producer
of The Goon Show, was first told of
Spike by a colleague during a recording of
Hip Hip Hoo Roy, who said, 'That's Spike
Milligan. Whenever [Derek Roy] uses one
of his gags, he laughs').

Much of the material Spike wrote for
that programme was never used, which is
hardly surprising really, as many of the
people on whom Spike tried out his early
jokes simply weren't ready for his style of
humour and didn't understand it.
Someone who did laugh at the jokes was
Peter Sellers, confirming to Spike that his
ideas and brand of comedy were viable –
and also that it was time for a change in
what was available as entertainment.
Thus the original fusion of Goons and
shared comedy ideas began to grow.

The nucleus of the Goons remained
Spike, Peter, Harry and Michael, although
others who shared the Grafton's orbit and
became significantly enthused about this
new line of comedy acquired a kind of half-
association and became mentioned in
journalism of the time. Bandwagon

'Mankind is a Goon' – Spike's
Theory of Irrelativity.

Magazine and The Performer printed features on this new grouping in October
and November 1949, naming amongst the 'Lesser Goons' Alfred Marks and Dick
Emery. At around the same time, Michael's solo theatre performances were
being reported in magazines such as Picturegoer under titles like 'The Original
Goon.'

The attitude that underpinned Goon ideas and comedy found one expression
in another early magazine article, clearly building on their shared wartime
experiences. What Spike coined as his 'Theory of Irrelativity' stated 'How would
I describe a Goon? Mankind is a Goon – anyone who can get a perfectly quiet
planet into such a bloody state in 2,000 years must indeed be a GOON.'

The early dynamics of Goon ideas were wild, lively, unpredictable – having little

Round and About Goonland

with Sidney Vauneez

LATEST COMIC ERUPTION in the Variety world is the blast caused by a highly intelligent bunch of synthetic crackpots who call themselves "Goons." I was in Peter Sellers' dressing-room on the night of his Palladium opening when one of the customary good-luck wires arrived. It read: "I am instructed by the Goon Council to forward the following message of congratulation. Quote: Ooly-Dooly-Osh. Unquote. P.S. Ool. Signed KOGVOS."

Alfred Marks got a similar wire when he opened in "Panama" at Brighton, so did Michael Bentine on the first night of "Folies Bergère." All three comedians are recognised Goons. Osh is their pass-word, Ool a roving noun used by them in practically any connotation; their favourite game is Goon-sequences, their theme song "Goon Songs at Eventide," their chosen radio listening "The Thud Programme," their top show "Annie Get Your Goon" and required reading "Goon With The Wind."

Goon-sequences is played with a home recorder. Each Goon tells part of a story and passes only the last word on to the next speaker. When half-a-dozen Goons have goon to town with the English language, the recording is played back and they hear for the first time what the others have said, shrieked, chirruped or mumbled. But they never play the recording through backwards—otherwise, they say, it might make sense, which would be unpardonable Gawkery and fit only for a Clerd—the strongest Goon form of disparagement.

Yet these Goons aren't as daffy as they sound. Their headquarters is in a resplendent West End pub, and more resplendent still Kogvos—short for Keeper of Goons and Voice of Sanity—owns it. Kogvos, alias Jimmy Douglas, the script-writer, is in private life a very staid, right thinking publican. But Goonery is for that very busy man, an ideal form of relaxation. His function amongst the Goons is to interpret their inspired insanity, to act as a link between them and the outside world. Goonism, he maintains, is a form of slap-stick expressed through surrealistic media. It is a delicate appreciation of the ridiculous, pointed in literature by Leacock, Thurber and Benchley, and in cartoons by artists like Ronnie Searle and Emmett.

There are now Goons, Lesser Goons, Goons Initiate and Goon Followers. They have their own peanut-silk tie and peanut-head badges. But it began in the army, with Harry Seacombe and Spike Milligan who toured the camps doing troop shows and practised Goonery among themselves in the barracks to get away from the deadly monotony of army life. They didn't talk to each other, they simply made weird noises and grimaces. "After all," says Spike, "Why talk? Why speak words?— Everyone speaks words!"

Goons recognise each other immediately. They all have a fundamental humorous quirk that betrays itself to kindred spirit. That is the essence of Goonery, a product of inspiration, not imitation. When Harry Seacombe started at the Windmill, he met Michael Bentine and reported to Spike—"There's a Goon if ever I saw one!" So Bentine was inducted in the circle, and then another

Peter Sellers points a pistol to end it all. But he is strung up by his necktie to get a flying start. And King Alfred Marks fiddles with his 'cello while his scones are burning

Sidney Vauneez was one of the first to try and explain the Goons' style of comedy.

in common with the established acts on stage and radio. Meeting up at Grafton's, under the continued benign guidance of Jimmy Grafton as KOGVOS ('King of Goons and Voice of Sanity'), led to informal performances of Goon sketches to pub audiences, as well as to Jimmy Grafton's wire recording machine.

'Ours was a kind of anarchy in comedy,' Harry recalled. 'We were against the established form of presentation. At the time we began, the profession was full of stand-up comics who came on and told a string of jokes and finished either with a song or dance. Our approach was different. We spent the war with lads of our own age in the Services and we had fresh ideas. . .'

Jimmy Grafton himself vividly describes one such moment, recorded spontaneously, called War Report. '[It was] a series of battle commentaries from various

Spike agrees terms.

who sees too much. Mop-haired Michael a fugitive from the Folies Bergère, with ligan fitting another ping to his bow

fronts together with appropriate vocal sound effects. Each time the invention flagged, we fed in a few seconds of Percy Manchester singing 'The Green Fields of England'. When we played the whole thing back, the effect was hysterical. . .' It rapidly became clear that these were performers with material that could find a place on the airwaves if given a chance.

Creating the opportunity proved to be more difficult. Harry and Michael began to develop successful individual performing careers as the 1940s gradually came to an end, with occasional radio performances on Listen My Children and Third Division. Spike struggled somewhat, supplying comedy material when the opportunity presented itself, but otherwise gaining income as a musician for music hall turns whilst living in Jimmy Grafton's pub attic (until quite recently those selfsame attic walls were extensively adorned with original Milliganisms).

It wasn't until 1950 that a first attempt was made to get the Goons on the air. Peter's radio career continued to prosper, moving beyond simple impressions on Showtime to supporting characterisations on the Ted Ray Show (it was here that early Sellers voices such as Crystal Jollibottom were first heard) and Variety Bandbox. It therefore seemed logical to propose a programme idea around a known radio performer. Thus began the idea for Sellers Castle,

Spike and Harry with some lesser Goons.

designed to feature Peter as Lord Sellers, Michael as a lunatic inventor and Harry as the singing protégé of 'lesser Goon' Alfred Marks, with Spike contributing characters as needed. Other 'regulars' from the Grafton circle participated as supporting cast and, when it came to preparing a professional pilot tape, the voice of BBC announcer Andrew Timothy (who knew Grafton from the War) was sought to link enough script excerpts to convey the essential 'feel' of the programme.

Coincidentally, it was again Roy Speer who was contacted by Jimmy Grafton and who commissioned a full-blown pilot on the basis of what he heard and read of the scripting. Fate then intervened with the appointment to the pilot programme not of Roy Speer, but rather one Jacques Brown. Jacques had previously produced Danger Men At Work, but had worked only within a studio setting – he did not tend to use audiences as an ingredient of the atmosphere of a radio comedy show.

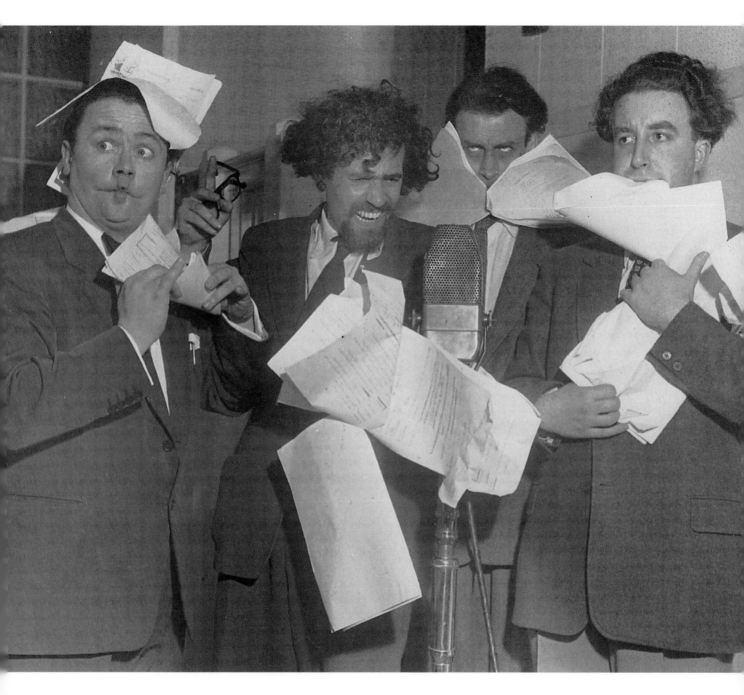

Recording.

Consequently, the full pilot was recorded without audience, on the under-standing that it would be listened to by the cast and adapted as necessary prior to full recording with a studio audience. Once that first recording was 'in the can', however, Jacques unilaterally decided it was acceptable to present to the BBC planners and submitted it without further consultation. The planners turned it down.

Failure led to months of lobbying different producers in the BBC, in the hopes of gaining another opportunity. Peter and Harry appeared on Variety Bandbox together in January 1950 and were referred to as 'Goons'. Eventually Peter managed to bring some samples of dialogue recorded with Spike to the attention of Pat Dixon. Pat was known as a radical within the BBC hierarchy and a bit of a firebrand – when he backed an idea it was difficult, if not impos-sible to stop it. Pat supported this idea and the Goons got their chance with another pilot recording on 4th February 1951.

THE DREADED BATTER PUDDING HURLER
(of Bexhill-on-Sea)

The Goon Show: No. 102 (5th Series, No. 3)
Transmission: Tuesday 12 October 1954
8.30-9.00 p.m. Home Service. Studio: Paris Cinema, London

The main characters

Mr Henry Crun	Peter Sellers
Miss Minnie Bannister	Spike Milligan
Ned Seagoon	Harry Secombe
Lance Brigadier Grytpype-Thynne	Peter Sellers
Sergeant Throat	Spike Milligan
Major Denis Bloodnok	Peter Sellers
Eccles	Spike Milligan
Odium	Spike Milligan
Moriarty	Spike Milligan
Willium	Peter Sellers
Bluebottle	Peter Sellers

The Ray Ellington Quartet
Max Geldray
Orchestra Conducted by Wally Stott
Announcer: Wallace Greenslade
Script by Spike Milligan. Production by Peter Eton

moriarty

How young Ned Seagoon was called in by the terrorised gentlefolk of of Bexhill to help track down the dreaded Batter Pudding Hurler. Striking when least expected, the 'Hurler' caused such havoc during the blackout of 1941 that troops, massed against the German invasion, were ordered to join the hunt. A trail of cold Batter Puddings eventually led Ned Seagoon to North Africa where, with the aid of Major Bloodnok, he finally cornered the traitor...

BILL   This is the BBC Home Service.

F.X.   PENNY IN MUG

BILL   Thank you. We now come to the radio show entirely dedicated to the downfall of John Snagge.

HARRY   He refers, of course, to the highly esteemed Goon Show.

GRAMS   SORROWFUL MARCH WITH WAILS

HARRY   Stop! Time for laughs later - but now to business. Mr Greenslade?   Come over here.

F.X.   CHAINS.

BILL   Yes, Master?

HARRY   Tell the waiting world what we have for them.

THE DREADED BATTER PUDDING HURLER (of Bexhill-on-sea)

BILL	My lords, ladies and other National Assistance holders - tonight the League of Burmese Trombonists presents a best-seller play entitled:
ORCHESTRA	TYMPANY ROLL. HELD UNDER:-
PETER	The Terror of Bexhill-on-Sea or . . .
ORCHESTRA	THREE DRAMATIC CHORDS.
HARRY	The Dreaded Batter Pudding Hurler.
ORCHESTRA	CLIMAX. THEN DOWN NOW BEHIND:-
BILL	The English Channel 1941. Across the silent strip of green-grey water – in England – coastal towns were deserted, except for people. Despite the threat of invasion and the stringent blackout rules, elderly gentlefolk of Bexhill-on-Sea still took their evening constitutionals.

F.X.	EBB TIDE ON A GRAVEL BEACH.
CRUN	Ohhh - it's quite windy on these cliffs.
MINNIE	What a nice summer evening - typical English.
CRUN	Mnk yes - the rain's lovely and warm - I think I'll take one of my sou' westers off - here, hold my elephant gun.
MINNIE	I don't know what you brought it for - you can't shoot elephants in England.
CRUN	Mnk? Why not?
MINNIE	They're out of season.
CRUN	Does this mean we'll have to have pelican for dinner again?
MINNIE	Yes, I'm afraid so.
CRUN	Then I'll risk it. I'll shoot an elephant out of season.
BOTH	(Go off mumbling in the distance)
BILL	Listeners who are listening will, of course, realise that Minnie and Henry are talking rubbish - as erudite people will realise, there are no elephants in Sussex. They are only found in Kent North on a straight line drawn between two points thus making it the shortest distance.
F.X.	PENNY IN MUG

BILL   Thank you

CRUN   . . . well, if that's how it is I can't shoot any.

MINNIE   Come Henry, we'd better be getting home. I don't want to be caught on the
            beaches if there's an invasion.

CRUN   Neither do I. I'm wearing a dirty shirt and I – mnk – don't –

F.X.   CLANK OF IRON OVEN DOOR

CRUN   . . . Minnie?

MINNIE   What what?

CRUN   Did you hear a gas oven door slam just then?

MINNIE   Don't be silly, Henry – who'd be walking around these cliffs with a gas oven?

CRUN   Lady Docker

Minnie Bannister

MINNIE   Yes, but apart from the obvious ones – who'd want to . . .

F.X.   WHOOSH - SPLOSH - BATTER PUDDING HITTING MINNIE

MINNIE   Oooooooooooohohohohohohohohohohohohohohohohoohohohoho . . .

CRUN   No, I've never heard of him.

MINNIE   Help, Henry – I've been struck down from behind. Help.

CRUN	Mnk – oh dear dear. (Calls) Police – English Police – Law Guardians???
MINNIE	Not too loud, Henry, they'll hear you.
F.X.	POLICE WHISTLE
SEAGOON	(approaching) Can I help you, sir?
CRUN	Are you a policeman?

SEAGOON	No, I'm a constable.
CRUN	What's the difference?
SEAGOON	They're spelt differently.
MINNIE	Ohhhhhhh.
SEAGOON	Oh! What's happened to this dear old silver-bearded lady?
CRUN	She was struck down from behind.
SEAGOON	And not a moment too soon – congratulations, sir.
CRUN	I didn't do it.
EAGOON	Coward – hand back your OBE. Now tell me who did this felonous deed. What's happened to her?

THE DREADED BATTER PUDDING HURLER (of Bexhill-on-sea)

CRUN	It's too dark to see – strike a light.
SEAGOON	Not allowed in blackout.
MINNIE	Strike a dark light.
SEAGOON	No madam, we daren't. Why, only twenty-eight miles across the Channel the Germans are watching this coast.
CRUN	Don't be a silly-pilly policeman. They can't see a little match being struck.
SEAGOON	Oh, all right.
F.X.	MATCH STRIKING – QUICK WHOOSH OF SHELL – SHELL EXPLODES.
SEAGOON	Any questions?
CRUN	Yes – where are my legs?
SEAGOON	Are you now aware of the danger from German long-range guns?
CRUN	Mnk ahh! I've got it – I have the answer. Just by chance I happen to have on me a box of German matches
SEAGOON	Wonderful – strike one. They won't fire at their own matches.
CRUN	Of course not - now . . .
F.X.	MATCH STRIKING AND FLARING – WHOOSH OF SHELL – SHELL BURST.
CRUN	. . .Curse . . .the British!!!
SEAGOON	We tried using a candle, but it wasn't very bright and we daren't light it - so we waited for dawn - and there, in the light of the morning sun, we saw what had struck Miss Bannister. It was - a Batter Pudding.
ORCHESTRA	DRAMATIC CHORD
CRUN	It's still warm, Minnie.
MINNIE	Thank Heaven - I hate cold Batter Pudding.
CRUN	Come, Minnie, I'll take you home - give you a hot bath - rub you down with the anti-vapour rub - put a plaster on your back - give your feet a mustard bath, and then put you to bed.
SEAGOON	Do you know this woman?
CRUN	Devilish man – of course I do – this is Minnie Bannister, the world-famous poker player. Give her a good poker and she'll play any tune you like.
SEAGOON	Well, get her off this cliff, it's dangerous. Meantime, I must report this to the Inspector. I'll call on you later - goodbye.
F.X.	(PAUSE) DISTANT SPLASH

SEAGOON   As I swam ashore I dried myself to save time. That night I lay awake
           in my air-conditioned dustbin thinking – who on earth would want to strike
           another with a Batter Pudding? Obviously it wouldn't happen again, so I fell
           asleep. Nothing much happened that night – except that I was struck with a
           Batter Pudding.

SPIKE   Mmmmm - it's all rather confusing, really.

BILL   In the months to come, thirty-eight Batter Puddings were hurled at
           Miss Bannister - a madman was at large - Scotland Yard were called in.

ORCHESTRA LINK.

G-T	(Sanders throughout) Inspector Seagoon - my name is Hercules Grytpype-Thynne, Special Investigation. This Batter Pudding Hurler-
SEAGOON	Yes?
G-T	He's made a fool of the police.
SEAGOON	I disagree - we were fools long before he came along.
G-T	You silly twisted boy. Nevertheless, he's got to be stopped - now, Seagoon -
SEAGOON	Yes yes yes yes yes yes?
G-T	. . . Please don't do that. Now, these Batter Puddings – they were obviously thrown by hand.
SEAGOON	Not necessarily – some people are pretty clever with their feet.
G-T	For instance?
SEAGOON	Tom Cringingknutt.
G-T	Who's he?
SEAGOON	He's a man who's pretty clever with his feet.
G-T	What's his name?
SEAGOON	Jim Phlatcrok.
G-T	Sergeant Throat?
THROAT	Sir?
G-T	Make a note of that.
THROAT	Right. Anything else?
G-T	Yes.
THROAT	Right.
G-T	Good. Now Seagoon, these Batter Puddings - were they all identical?
SEAGOON	All except this last one. Inside it - we found this.
G-T	Oh! An Army Boot! So the Dreaded Hurler is a military man. Any troops in the town?
SEAGOON	The fifty-sixth Heavy Underwater Artillery.
G-T	Get there at once - arrest the first soldier you see wearing one boot.
SEAGOON	Ying tong iddle I po.
G-T	Right - off you go.
ORCHESTRA	BLOODNOK SIGNATURE TUNE.
BLOODNOK	Bleiough – aeioughhh – bleioughhhh – how dare you come here to my H.Q. with such an –
SEAGOON	I tell you, Major Bloodnok, I must ask you to parade your men.
BLOODNOK	Why?

SEAGOON	I'm looking for a criminal.
BLOODNOK	You find your own - it took me years to get this lot.
SEAGOON	Ying tong iddle I po.
BLOODNOK	Very well then – Bugler Max Geldray? Sound fall in – the hard way.
MAX & ORCHESTRA	THEY WERE DOING THE MAMBO
	(Applause)
ORCHESTRA & CAST	(Murmers of distrust)
BLOODNOK	Silence, lads! I'm sorry I had to get you out of bed in the middle of the day - but I'll see you get extra pay for this.
ORCHESTRA & CAST	You flat 'eaded kipper - Gawn, drop dead – I'll claht yer flippin' head - Gorn, shimmer orf.
BLOODNOK	Ahhhhhhh, that's what I like, spirit. Now, Seagoon -– which is the man?
SEAGOON	I walked among the ranks looking for the soldier with one boot but my luck was out: the entire regiment were barefooted – all save the officers, who wore reinforced concrete socks.
BLOODNOK	Look Seagoon, it's getting dark. You can't see in this light.
SEAGOON	I'll strike a match.
F.X.	MATCH...WHOOSH OF SHELL EXPLOSION.
SEAGOON	Curse, I forgot about the Germans.
ECCLES	We want our beddy byes.
SEAGOON	Who are you?
ECCLES	Lance Private Eccles, but most people call me by my nick-name.
SEAGOON	What's that?
ECCLES	Hahum. Nick.
SEAGOON	I inspected the man closely – he was the nearest thing I'd seen to a human being, without actually being one.
BLOODNOK	Surely you don't suspect this man – why, we were together in the same company during that terrible disaster.

SEAGOON	What company was that?
BLOODNOK	Desert Song 1933.
SEAGOON	Were you both in the D'Oyly Carte?
BLOODNOK	Right in the D'Oyly Carte.
SEAGOON	I don't wish to know that, but wait!! At last – by the light of a passing glue factory – I saw that Eccles was only wearing – one boot!
ECCLES	Well, I only got one boot.
SEAGOON	I know – but why are you wearing it on your head?
ECCLES	Why? It fits, dat's why – what a silly question – why – why –
SEAGOON	Let me see that boot. (Sotto) Mmmm, size nineteen . . . (Aloud) What size head have you got?
ECCLES	Size nineteen.
SEAGOON	Curse – the man's defence was perfect – Major Bloodnok?
BLOODNOK	How dare you call me Major Bloodnok.
SEAGOON	That's your name.
BLOODNOK	In that case – I forgive you.
SEAGOON	Where's this man's other boot?
BLOODNOK	Stolen.
SEAGOON	Who by?
BLOODNOK	A thief.
SEAGOON	You sure it wasn't a pickpocket?
BLOODNOK	Positive – Eccles never keeps his boots in his pocket.
SEAGOON	Damn. They all had a watertight alibi – but just to make sure I left it in a fish tank overnight. Next morning my breast pocket phone rang.
F.X.	RING.
SEAGOON	Hello?
CRUN	Mr. Seagoon – Minnie's been hit with another Batter Pudding.
SEAGOON	Well, that's nothing new.
CRUN	It was – this one was stone cold.
SEAGOON	Cold???
CRUN	Yes – he must be losing interest in her.
SEAGOON	It proves also that the phantom Batter Pudding Hurler has had his gas-pipe cut off! Taxi!
F.X.	BAGPIPES. RUNNING DOWN.
SPIKE	Yes?

SEAGOON	The Bexhill Gas Works, and step on it.
SPIKE	Yes.
F.X.	BAGPIPES. FADE OFF.
BILL	Listeners may be puzzled by a taxi sounding like bagpipes. The truth is – it is all part of the BBC new economy campaign. They have discovered that it is cheaper to travel by bagpipes – not only are they more musical, but they come in a wide variety of colours. See your local bagpipe offices and ask for particulars – you won't be disappointed.
SPIKE	It's all rather confusing, really ...
PETER	Meantime, Neddie Seagoon had arrived at the Bexhill Gas and Coke Works.
SEAGOON	Phewwwwww blimeyyyyy – anyone about?
ODIUM	Yererererere.
SEAGOON	Good.
ODIUM	Yerrer.
SEAGOON	I'd like a list of people who haven't paid their gas bills.
ODIUM	Yererererere -
SEAGOON	Oh, thank you. Now here's a good list – I'll try this number.
F.X.	DIALLING.
SEAGOON	Think we've got him this time – hello?
PETER	(Winston Churchill – distort) Ten Downing Street here.
SEAGOON	(gulp) I'm sorry.
F.X.	CLICK
SEAGOON	No, it couldn't be him – who would he want to throw a Batter Pudding at?
F.X.	QUICK 'PHONE RING
SEAGOON	Hello? Police here.
SPIKE	This is Mr Attlee – someone's just thrown a Batter Pudding at me.
ORCHESTRA	TYMPANY ROLL HELD UNDER NEXT SPEECH:-
SEAGOON	Months went by – still no sign of the Dreaded Hurler. Finally I walked the streets of Bexhill at night disguised as a human man – then suddenly!!
ORCHESTRA	FLARING CHORD.
SEAGOON	Nothing happened. But it happened suddenly. Disappointed, I lit my pipe.

Neddie Seagoon

F.X.   MATCH. WHOOSH OF SHELL. EXPLOSION OF SHELL.

SEAGOON   Curse those Germans.

MORIARTY   Pardon me, my friend.

SEAGOON   I turned to see the speaker – he was a tall man wearing sensible feet   and a head to match. He was dressed in the full white outfit of a Savoy chef – around his waist were tied several thousand cooking instruments – behind him he pulled a portable gas stove from which issued forth the smell of Batter Pudding.

MORIARTY   Could I borrow a match? You see, my gas has gone out and my Batter Pudding was just browning.

SEAGOON   Certainly. Here – no – keep the whole box – I have another match at home.

MORIARTY   So rich. Well, thank you, m'sieur – you have saved my Batter Pudding from getting cold. There's nothing worse than being struck down with a cold Batter Pudding.

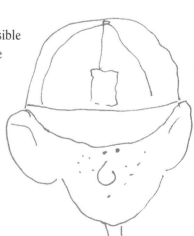

Blue bottle

SEAGOON	Oh yes.
MORIARTY	Good night.
SEAGOON	I watched the strange man as he pulled his gas stove away into the darkness. But I couldn't waste time watching him – my job was to find the Dreaded Batter Pudding Hurler.
BILL	Those listeners who think that Seagoon is not cut out to be a detective – please write to him care of Rowton House.
SEAGOON	On December 25th the Hurler changed his tactics – that day Miss Bannister was struck with a Christmas Pudding. Naturally, I searched the workhouse.
WILLIUM	No sir – we ain't had no Christmas puddin' here, have we mate?
SPIKE	No.
WILLIUM	We ain't had none for three years, have we mate?
SPIKE	No – it's all rather annoying, really.
CRUN	(approaching) Ahh Mr Sniklecrum ...
MINNIE	Ahhhhh
SEAGOON	Mr Crun, Miss Bannister, what are you doing here?
CRUN	Mnk, Minnie had a letter this morning.
MINNIE	I had a letter.
CRUN	Mn gnup ... I'll tell him Minnie.
MINNIE	Thank you, Henry.
CRUN	Mnk – yes, she had a –
MINNIE	Yes, you tell him.
CRUN	All right, I'll tell . . .
MINNIE	. . . Yes . . .
CRUN	She had a lett ...
SEAGOON	Yes, I know she had a letter – what about it?
CRUN	It proves that the Batter Pudding Hurler is abroad.
SEAGOON	What? Why? How?
CRUN	It was post-marked Africa – and inside was a portion of Batter Puddin'.
MINNIE	Yes – he hasn't forgotten me.
SEAGOON	So he's in Africa – now we've got him cornered. I must leave at once. Bluebottle!
B'BOTTLE	I heard you call, my captain – I heard my captain call – waits for audience applause – not a sausage – puts on I don't care expression as done by Aneurin Bevan at Blackpool Conservative Rally.
SEAGOON	Bluebottle – you and I are going to Africa.

THE DREADED BATTER PUDDING HURLER (of Bexhill-on-sea)

B'BOTTLE	Good – can we take sandwiches?
SEAGOON	Only for food – any questions?
B'BOTTLE	No.
SEAGOON	I can't answer that – can you?
B'BOTTLE	No.
SEAGOON	Ignorant swine. Got that down, Sergeant Throat?
THROAT	Yes.
SEAGOON	Good.
THROAT	Yes.
SEAGOON	Right, we catch the very next troop convoy to Algiers. And who better to drive us out of the country than Ray Ellington and his Quartet?
QUARTET	'OL' MAN RIVER'.
(Applause)	
ORCHESTRA	'VICTORY AT SEA' THEME.
PETER	And now ...
F.X.	WASH OF THE WAVES ON SHIP'S PROW.
BILL	Seagoon and Bluebottle travelled by sea. To avoid detection by enemy U-boats they spoke German throughout the voyage, heavily disguised as Spaniards.
PETER	As an added precaution they travelled on separate decks and wore separate shoes on different occasions.
SEAGOON	The ship was disguised as a train – to make the train sea-worthy it was done up to look like a boat and painted to appear like a tram.
SPIKE	. . . All rather confusing, really.
SEAGOON	Also on board were Major Bloodnok and his regiment. When we were ten miles from Algiers we heard a dreaded cry.
ECCLES	(off) Mine ahead – dreadful sea-mine ahead.
BLOODNOK	(approach) What's happening here – why are all these men cowering down on deck, the cowards?
SEAGOON	There's a mine ahead.
BLOODNOK	Mi –
F.X.	HURRIED FOOTSTEPS AWAY AND THEN SPLASH.
SEAGOON	Funny – he wasn't dressed for swimming.
ECCLES	Hey, dere's no need to worry about the mine.
B'BOTTLE	Yes, I must worry – I don't want to be deaded – I'm wearing my best sports shirt. (Hurriedly puts on cardboard tin hat.)

ECCLES	Don't worry – dat mine, it can't hurt us – it's one of ours.
F.X.	EXPLOSION
SEAGOON	Eccles, is the ship sinking?
ECCLES	Only below the sea.
SEAGOON	We must try and save the ship – help me get it into the lifeboat.
ECCLES	O.K. ... Upppppppp.
BOTH	(Grunts and groans)
ECCLES	It's no good, the ship won't fit into the lifeboat.
SEAGOON	What a ghastly oversight by the designer. Never mind, it leaves room for one more in the boat.
BLOODNOK	I'm willing to fill that vacancy.
SEAGOON	How did you get back on board?
BLOODNOK	I was molested by a lobster with a disgusting mind.
SEAGOON	Right, Bloodnok, do your duty.
BLOODNOK	(calls) Women and children first.
SEAGOON	Bloodnok, take that dummy out of your mouth.
ECCLES	Hey, don't leave me behind.
BLOODNOK	And why not?
ECCLES	... Give me time and I'll think of a reason.
BLOODNOK	Right, wait here until Apple Blossom Time – meantime, Seagoon, lower away.
F.X.	WINCHES GOING.
ECCLES	Hey – if you make room for me, I'll pay ten pounds.
F.X.	SPLASH.
SEAGOON	(off) You swine Bloodnok -
BLOODNOK	Business is business – get in, Eccles.
ECCLES	Ta.
SEAGOON	(off) Look, I'll pay twenty pounds for a place in the boat.
F.X.	SPLASH.
BLOODNOK	(off) Aeiough, you double-crosser, Eccles.
ECCLES	Get in, Captain Seagoon.
HARRY	Ahhh, thank you, Eccles – myyy friend.
BLOODNOK	(off) Thirty pounds for a place.
F.X.	SPLASH.
ECCLES	(off) You ain't my friend.

BLOODNOK	Ahhhh, good old Seagoon, you've saved me.
SEAGOON	My pal.
ECCLES	(off) Fifty pounds for a place in the boat.
F.X.	TWO DISTANT SPLASHES.
SPIKE	Alert listeners will have heard two splashes – this means that both Bloodnok and Seagoon have been hurled in the water – who could have done this?
B'BOTTLE	Ha heuheuheuheuheuhuh – I dood it I doo – I hid behind a tin of dry biscuits and then I grabbed their tootsies and upppp into the water – ha heheu huehhhh –
ECCLES	Bluebottle, you saved my life.
B'BOTTLE	O ha well, we all make mistakes! I like this game – what school do you go to?
ECCLES	Reform. (Both fading off)
SEAGOON	Tricked by the brilliant planning of Bluebottle and Eccles, Bloodnok and I floundered in the cruel sea.
F.X.	SEA.
BLOODNOK	Fortunately we found a passing lifeboat and dragged ourselves aboard.
SEAGOON	We had no oars but luckily we found two outboard motors and we rowed with them.
BLOODNOK	Brilliant.
SEAGOON	For thirty days we drifted to and fro – then hunger came upon us.

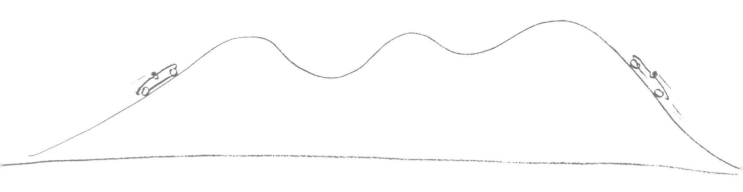

BLOODNOK	Aeioughhhhhhh – if I don't eat soon I'll die and if I die I won't eat soon. Wait – (snifffff) can I smell cooking or do my ears deceive me?
SEAGOON	He was right – he has smelly ears – something was cooking – there in the other end of the lifeboat was – a gas stove! Could this be the end of our search?
BLOODNOK	I'll knock on the oven door.
F.X.	KNOCKING ON OVEN DOOR.
MORIARTY	(off) Just a minute, I'm in the bath ... (Pause)
F.X.	COMING DOWN IRON STAIRS. MORIARTY SINGING. OVEN DOOR OPENS.
MORIARTY	Good morning – I'm sorry – you!!!
SEAGOON	Yes – remember Bexhill – I lent you the matches.
MORIARTY	You don't want them back?
SEAGOON	Don't move – I arrest you as the Dreaded Batter Pudding Hurler. Hands up, you devil – don't move – this finger is loaded.
MORIARTY	If you kill me I promise you will never take me alive.
BLOODNOK	Wait – how can we prove it?
SEAGOON	That Batter Pudding in the corner of the stove is all the evidence we need. We've got him.
ORCHESTRA	CRASHING TRIUMPHANT THEME.
F.X.	QUIET SEA. LAPPING OF WAVES.
BILL	But it wasn't easy – forty days they drifted in an open boat.
FIDDLE	'HEARTS AND FLOWERS'.
BLOODNOK	Oooaeioughhh, I tell you Seagoon – let's eat the Batter Pudding or we'll starve!!

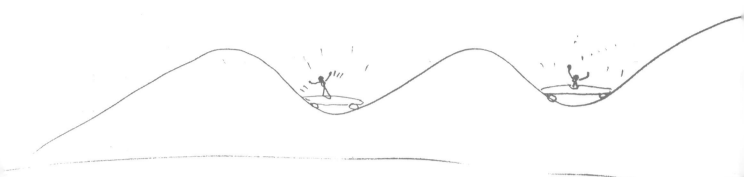

SEAGOON	No, d'yer hear me – no! That's the only evidence we've got – though I must admit this hunger does give one an appetite.
BLOODNOK	We must eat it or die.
SEAGOON	Never!!!
BLOODNOK	We must.
BOTH	(Fade off)
BILL	And that, we fear, is the end of our story except, of course, for the end – we invite listeners to submit what they think should be the classic ending. Should Seagoon eat the Batter Pudding and live or leave it and in the cause of justice – die? Meantime, for those of you cretins who would like a happy ending – here it is.
GRAMS	SWEET BACKGROUND MUSIC, VERY, VERY SOFT.
HARRY	Darling – darling, will you marry me?
BLOODNOK	Of course I will – darling.
BILL	Thank you – good night.
ORCHESTRA	SIGNATURE TUNE: UP AND DOWN FOR :
BILL	That was The Goon Show – a recorded programme featuring Peter Sellers, Harry Secombe and Spike Milligan with the Ray Ellington Quartet and Max Geldray. The Orchestra was conducted by Wally Stott. Script by Spike Milligan. Announcer: Wallace Greenslade. The programme produced by Peter Eton.
ORCHESTRA	SIGNATURE TUNE UP TO END.
(Applause)	
MAX & ORCHESTRA	'CRAZY RHYTHM' PLAYOUT.

SPIKE MILLIGAN'S STORY

'Do you know there were only three women who appeared in the Goon Show? The first was Margaret McMillan, a classy girl. I was going out with her at the time.'

Spike Milligan's recollections about his experiences on the Goon Show are typically direct and involve the real people who were involved with The Goons more than they do theories about the evolution of a classic comedy show.

'The girls appeared from time to time according to who was dating them. Peter Sellers had one. Her name was Charlotte Greenwood and I wrote a line for him to say to her "you're a dull scrubber". Peter said, "I can't say that to Charlotte, I'm going out with her!"'

'There was another girl, a little girl she was, who was hopelessly in love with Peter. She had a little voice like this: "No, no, no, I don't think I could do that!" I forget her name. I'm grateful I have forgotten her name.

'That's as far as the women went - Harry never brought a woman in. I think he was terrified of Myra [his wife] getting to know. Yes, there were only three women in all the Goon Shows. Not many people know that. The show was free of women after that. Thank God. They didn't gel, I think.

'There were female characters, though. There was Maid Marion, who was an Olympic pole vaulter. Robin Hood had fallen in the water and couldn't swim. Robin yells, "Help! Help! Help! I can't swim!" and a voice yells back, "I can't play the trombone, but I don't tell everybody about it!" When Robin is dying he fires an arrow and says, "I want to buried where it lands," and it lands in a ham-

Spike in a relaxed pose late in 1959, contemplating the end of the Goon Shows.

Top: Party time in the back room of the Grafton Arms.

Above: Spike shares a sausage with actress June Thorburn, 1962.

burger.'

Having strayed but a bow shot away from real people, Spike's early memories of those who were involved turn to publican and radio scriptwriter Jimmy Grafton, who was a huge source of inspiration and encouragement for the fledgling Goons when they first came together just a couple of years after the end of World War II.

'Jimmy had been an officer in the army and when we first met he was writing scripts for a comic called Derek Roy who was about as funny as a baby dying with cancer - and the jokes were also dying of cancer. He asked me to join him and to put some jokes in. But Derek Roy didn't understand my jokes so he would leave them out. My contribution to radio at that time was for him not to use me or my jokes but I went on writing them. I was paid £3 or £4 for him not using my jokes and continued writing for this remuneration. Yes - writing jokes in the attic.'

The attic in question was above Jimmy Grafton's pub in the Victoria area of

London, which conjures up the image of a struggling artist toiling away in his garrett all alone, but Spike discovered he had a neighbour . . .

'I have no idea why, but the attic was in three sections and I was in one with my typewriter. I used to hear a noise in the attic next door. I looked through the keyhole, and there was a monkey looking back at me through the keyhole. Later on the monkey bit me, so they locked it in the garage.'

Spike's time spent eaking out unperformed scripts on his old typewriter would not go to waste but, having survived the attack of the attic dwelling monkey, there was worse in store for him when he ventured downstairs.

'In the early days, all those scripts that were being written for Derek Roy and being left out were building up a store of left-out jokes in my mind. It was about this time that I met a man whom I had first met in Italy in the soldiers' concert party when he was a Polish comic. I discovered he was a Welsh comic called Harry Secombe but I went on thinking of him as a Polish comic because I couldn't understand a bloody word he said.

'I thought he was on some kind of speed, so much so that at the end of his act I felt he should have exploded and disappeared in a cloud of smoke - and I still believe that.'

Spike knew Harry from the days when Spike played with a musical comedy group. The group appeared in a show which included Harry as a comic, touring Italy entertaining troops towards the end of the war. It was while he was playing in this strange group that Spike first realised that he could make an audience laugh.

'I was a guitar player in the Bill Hall Trio in Italy. We used to play hot jazz and all dressed in rags. I used to tell jokes between numbers. They were as bad

Harry and Spike at the Grafton Arms with Johnny, the monkey, which Jimmy Grafton bought as a present for his wife.

Spike playing guitar with the
Bill Hall Trio in Italy.

as this - "And now the unfinished symphony, which we are going to finish!" That was the level of the jokes.'

When Harry was demobbed, he headed home, but Spike stayed on, performing with the Bill Hall Trio until they were eventually transported back to England.

It was shortly after Spike's reunion with the unexploded Welshman that he was introduced to Peter Sellers.

'Peter wanted to look like a male model - posh suit, posh collar and tie, macintosh, gloves he carried in his left hand . . . oh, and a trilby hat. I met him at the Hackney Empire. He was waiting for somebody who apeared to be a Polish comic. Peter was very softly spoken – I thought I was going deaf! I was very impressed by his countenance. He was quite dignified, apart from the fact that he didn't buy a bloody drink all night. Dignified but skint. Eventually he did put his hand in his pocket and pulled out a handkerchief. The Polish comic joined us at the bar and proceeded to spend his entire night's takings on alcohol for me and Peter.'

There was, of course, a fourth member of this pre-Goons alliance, a man with an extraordinarily chequered background – or was he perhaps just a mischievous teller of tall tales?

'Later we encountered a lunatic in the shape of a man called Michael Bentine who, according to himself, had wrestled in hand-to-hand combat with a German paratrooper and flew bombers with a Polish navigator who couldn't understand English. Consequently, they crashed into the hills and as a result he had a silver plate in his head. I wonder what he had last eaten off it?

'He once told me, face to face, that his mother had levitated from the ground, across the dining table and settled down on the other side. One night in Birmingham I asked him, as he was a mathematician, could he give me the formula for the atom bomb? He took out a lipstick and covered the mirror in the dressing room with Pythagoras and he finished off at the bottom right-hand side: "There, that is the formula for the atom bomb."

'Unfortunately, Professor Penny happened to be in the audience that night and he was a friend of mine. He came into the dressing room and looked at the mirror. I asked him what it was and he said, "That's a load of bollocks." I told Michael and he said, "Of course it is. You don't think I would give away the secret of the atom bomb in a dressing room, do you?"

'A mysterious man. With his death the world has lost a unique character and comic.'

Although the team was now together, performing and experimenting with tape recorders in The Grafton Arms, they needed a wider audience for the type of comedy they were developing. At that time, radio was the medium of mass entertainment and it was the BBC they had to target. The way in was through a BBC producer.

Peter admiring the shapely legs
of actress Avril Angers during
the making of Finckel's Café for
the BBC in 1956.

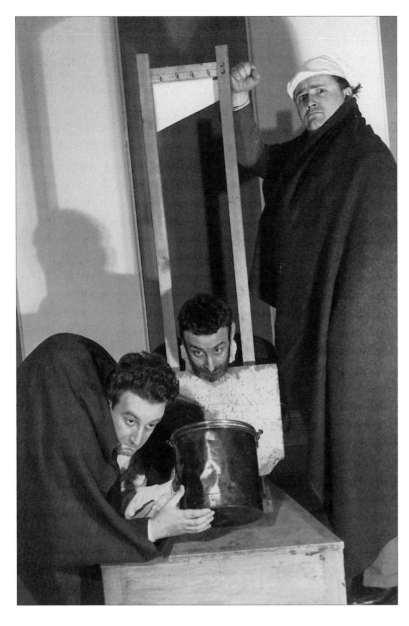

Spike is due for the chop as the Goons lark around for the cameras in 1953.

'Peter had a contact, a producer called Pat Dixon. He was an innovator. He did Breakfast with Braden, Bedtime with Braden, and Brass Hatters Band. Really, he didn't show much interest in us at first, but I think he felt there was a spark of talent that needed to be recognised, so I went away and wrote the crappiest script ever.'

The 'crappiest script ever' was enough to persuade the BBC that they had a fresh new style of comedy on their hands and Pat Dixon became the Goons' greatest ally in the corporation.

'Pat Dixon was marvellous. Do you know when Beachcomber was off, Pat would stand in for him. I remember when I was doing Beachcomber at the BBC, I invited Pat to lunch. Towards the end, he suddenly looked at his watch and said, "I've got to go, I feel a severe attack of British Railways coming on."

'He was a one-off. One thing that really hurt me was that when he died I wanted to do a show. I told the BBC I wanted to do an appreciation for him. They said no, as it would set a precedent.'

With Pat Dixon backing them up, the Goons were ready to take to the airwaves on the BBC, but not without a few minor hiccoughs.

'Do you know what they wanted to call us? The Junior Crazy Gang!'

From the very beginning, Spike wanted to call the show the Goon Show, and indeed it was as The Goons that the foursome were already making themselves known on the London comedy circuit.

'It was my idea for us to call ourselves The Goons. It was the name of the huge creatures in the Popeye cartoons who spoke in balloons with rubbish writing in them. The name certainly predates the beginning of the war. I started using the "Goons" in the army.'

The first Goon Shows would be billed as The Crazy People, but Spike's outrage at the titling of the show was a matter that would be settled later; first he had to take his script through the trauma of a performance in a BBC studio and as far as Spike remembers, it was the musicians who saved the day.

'Peter had been in recording studios before and so had Harry. I was the only one outside the pale. I didn't really think anything about it; I was so worried in case they didn't like the script. The audience didn't understand a word of it. God bless the band; they saved it. They all dug the jokes. They were

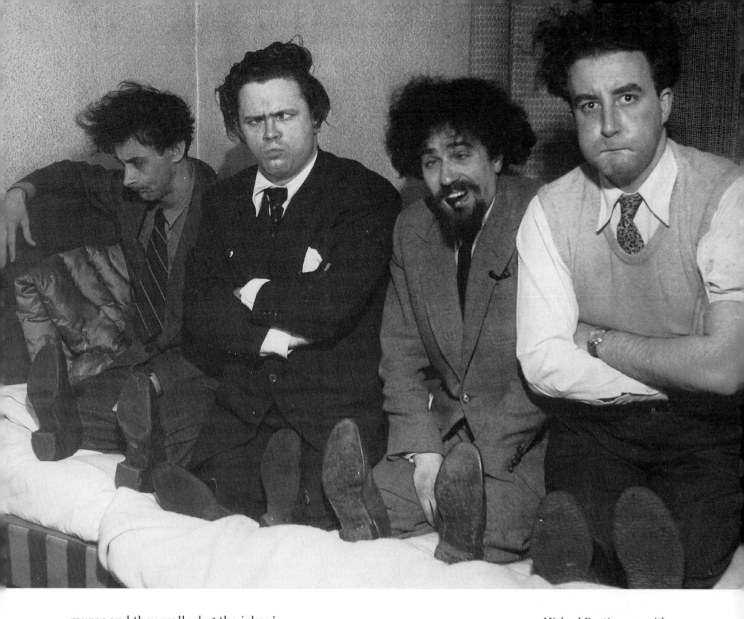

muzos and they really dug the jokes.'

The first broadcast of The Crazy People went out on 12th April 1951. It wasn't until the second season that Spike and the others would finally get their own way and the show was renamed the Goon Show. Despite the popularity of the show, however, there were always certain restrictions imposed on the Goons by the BBC.

'We could use a whole spectrum of voices. Peter could do anything from a dustman to the Queen and we could do lots of other voices we could have been a wow in the satirical field, but the BBC didn't like us doing voices like General Montgomery, Churchill or the Queen. They only accepted jokes like, "I used to play the Palladium." "Yes, I know. I've never heard it played better."'

The jokes, the sketches and the basic ideas for the scripts ultimately all came from Spike and, despite his dwindling store of 'left-out jokes', the pressure this brought to bear on him was immense.

'It all came from my fragmented

Michael Bentine was with the Goons in 1951 (above), but had firmly established his solo career by the time this shot was taken in 1960.

Spike using his bike to get around in 1959 and (below) waiting for inspiration in 1952.

fertile mind, I suppose. Most of it was locked up in my mind. I didn't know that that first show would be the first one of two-hundred shows. I didn't know there was that much in me. I sweated over it. I had to write one every week. I would write one and then I had to write another one in five days. It was an inborn spirit of pressure willing me on to my death.

'I was living in Finchley and I was going to the office in Shepherds Bush every day. I had to write to get away from the family. I got away from the kids falling all over me with jam, treacle, tapioca and rice pudding. I had to have a shower every morning before I could go out. Mind you, the kids were covered in jam, treacle, tapioca and rice pudding, so I went into the shower with all of them. I left home leaving them under the shower with the tap on, hoping eventually they would drown but when I got back at night they had survived and were ready to cover me with jam, treacle, tapioca, rice pudding, orange juice, lemonade and sometimes shit.'

Keeping up the constant stream of ideas and scripts which were required for the show took a heavy toll on Spike and certainly contributed to the health problems which ultimately led to his hospitalization.

'I suddenly had a breakdown. I had the AA tow me away to a psychiatric hospital. They didn't just keep me in, they kept the AA as well. This all really went back to the war when I was blown up. If I'd known what was good for me, I'd never have come down. Writing the show broke up my first marriage. I've just become normal again in the past four or five years with this drug called lithium.'

To help ease the pressure, Spike worked with a number of co-writers on the show including Larry Stephens, John Antrobus, Maurice Wiltshire and Eric Sykes, although the lion's share of the writing was still undertaken by Spike. Sykes was one of Spike's most important collaborators and became a close friend from the

moment they first met.

'I love Eric. It was either in a pub or a mental home where we first met and I got on with him straight away. You can't help but like him, you know. He is a formidable writer himself, having written 21 years of an award-winning series. Now most of that is gathering dust in the BBC archives, of course.'

Spike and Eric's friendship led to them working together on Archie In Goonland, a combination of the radio show Eric was writing, Educating Archie, and Spike's Goon Show. It was after Archie In Goonland that Eric became involved in writing some of the Goon Show scripts.

'We used to work together in Shepherds Bush above a greengrocers. Scruffy Dale, a rather dodgy entrepreneur used to let rooms there and I booked one of them. Galton and Simpson, John Antrobus, Johnny Speight and Terry Nation were in there as well. You had to be above something, this just happened to be a greengrocers.'

Although Sykes was the only writer to pen an entire show without any input from Milligan, he has always been quite adamant that all he was doing was copying a style created by Spike. Spike, on the other hand, pays tribute to Sykes's writing talents.

'I only ever cast an eye over the scripts Eric wrote. As I said, he is a formidable writer of a certain type of comedy. He is the best droll comedy writer we have. Yes, a certain type of comedy – middle of the road – he was covered in tyre marks.

'By comparison, Larry Stephens was small beer. He was never really a writer, I suppose. Larry would occasionally think of an idea, but by then the show was over.'

The Goons and Wallace Greenslade on stage in 1954 watched by Max Geldray in the background and Eric Sykes seated on the stage front right.

The Goons were persuaded to pose with a beautiful model as a publicity stunt . . .

Most successful radio or TV comedy shows have a team of writers bouncing ideas off each other to produce the laughs. While there were others who contributed to the Goons, Spike believes he worked best alone.

'My umbilical with life had been cut and I was floating in a womb of my own, revolving round and round with ideas spilling out of my head faster than I could catch them, grabbing at them.

'I suppose I should say that it was a wonderful experience but at the time I didn't seem to think so. I was so concerned with getting it all down on paper. The next line was all-important in the script I was writing and it had to be funny. When I was finished giving as many lines to one character as possible, I would switch to another character and Crun or Minnie Bannister would take up the story.'

So where did the inspiration come from for all this surreal humour? Was it in his genes?

'No, it was in my right leg. My dad was a clown and performing was in my blood. When my father heard the first Goon Show he said to my mother, "Thank God, I thought he'd never make it."

'We weren't like any other comedy act. Not even the Marx Brothers or W C Fields or the Ritz Brothers. At the time I admired Jacques Tati and a Canadian humourist called Stephen Leacock - he was very funny. I also liked Lear and Beachcomber.'

Jimmy Grafton worked as script editor on many of the Goon Shows and believed that the Goon characters, especially Eccles, were based on Spike's own character traits.

'That means I'm a full-time idiot! I don't quite think that I am at that level. Mind you, sometimes I break down and become Eccles – then I take a Valium.

Maybe Grafton was right, the bastard. I thought he was Eccles, actually. Why shouldn't he be? There could be two Eccleses. I could have a brother. Personally, I think the world is full of Eccleses, especially in New Zealand.'

The first Goon Shows were a collection of sketches interspersed with musical interludes. It wasn't until the third series that the shows became one three-part story. This was a development that Eric Sykes had been advising was a good idea and the arrival of producer Peter Eton made it a reality.

'Peter Eton came from drama and he formed the Goon Show into a sort of drama group. We had to have a story with a beginning, a middle and an end. One exciting story about Peter Eton comes from the Dover Lifeboats. We had a phone call from them saying that Peter had been dragged from the raging seas, drunk out of his mind, having fallen overboard from a channel steamer.

'He also managed to die in his lifetime and I miss him very much, like I did when he was alive. His wife is still alive and she often phones me to remind me that her husband is dead and, of course, I congratulate her. They call her squirrel – obviously because she's nuts.'

With the format for the show well-established, the three main protagonists (Bentine left after series two) settled into their roles. Their close friendship and Milligan's understanding of Secombe and Sellers' performance strengths creating a magic bond between them. To Spike's amazement, Sellers once described himself as '. . . just a vase of flowers, and Milligan arranged me.'

'Good God, that's a very poetic version of it. Wonderful symbolism, yes, or a complete bloody lie. There was a central spark, though, a sheer delight in good abstract comedy. We all loved it and couldn't wait for Sunday to come to give birth to that comedy, to hear an audience helpless with laughter. Secombe was pretty helpless, too. He'd drunk half a bottle of it by the time the show

. . . it could all have gone so terribly wrong!

ALL CROCKERY MUST BE RETURNED T THE COUNT

was finished.

'Harry was the central stabiliser, a married man successful in his relationship with his wife. He used to bring her flowers – and she ate them.

'Peter was a portable matress awaiting a companion. When they arrived he used to give them flowers – and he ate them. I was the permanent psychiatric patient, going into one psychiatric home after another.'

Music always played an important part in the shows, as interludes between sketches in the early days and later as a more integral part of the performances.

The show would not have been the same without Ray Ellington and Max Geldray, and Spike is a great admirer of them both.

'Ray and Max were both recruited by Pat Dixon, who was a jazz buff. They

The Goons had established themselves by the mid-1950s and opportunities to clown for the cameras came thick and fast.

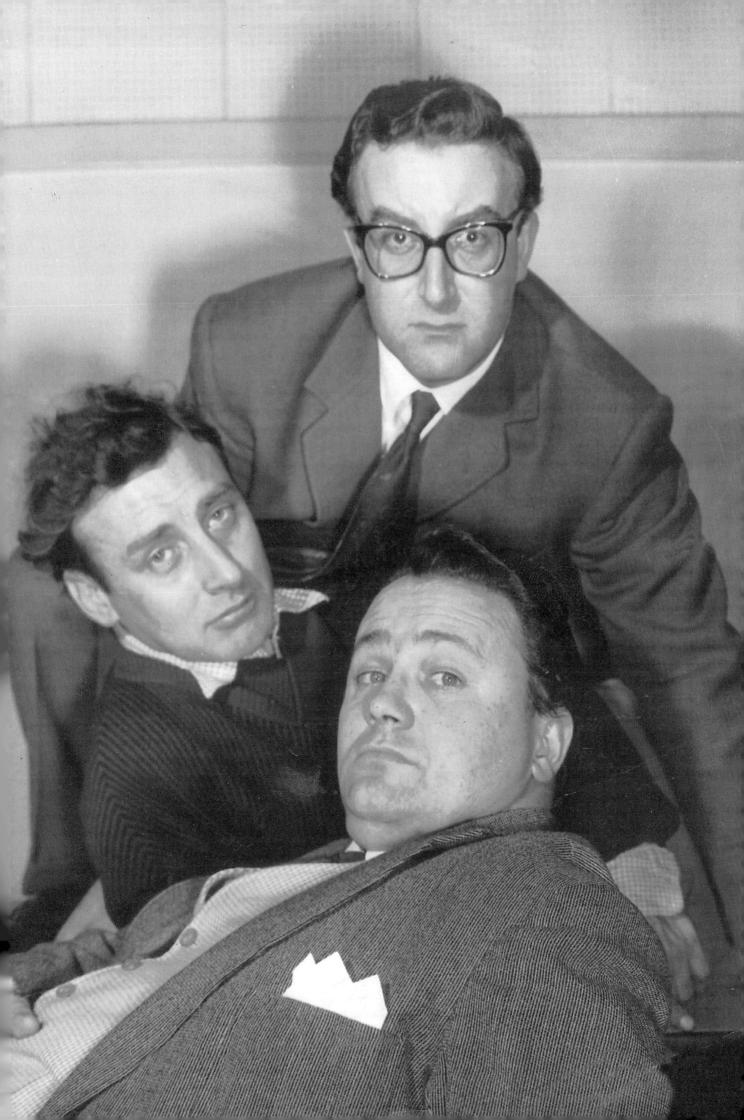

By the time this photo was taken in 1960, The Goon Show was gone, but the fun carried on . . .

were brought in especially for the Goon Show and they were both wonderful musicians.

'Wally Stott conducted the orchestra and wrote some exquisite themes for the Goons. They set the scene so well. He has now had a sex change. I don't know why. When he undresses he still looks like Wally Stott. A strange crowd of people were involved in the Goon Show.

'I think when Secombe undressed at night he looked like Wally Stott. Peter didn't. When he undressed at night he looked like Diana Dors. When Michael Bentine undressed at night he didn't look like anybody. I myself didn't get undressed at night.'

The announcer on the show became the butt of many of Spike's jokes. The original announcer was Andrew Timothy, but Spike best remembers the longer serving (and suffering) Wallace Greenslade.

'Wallace Greenslade was assigned to us by the Wallace Greenslade Assignor. He appeared unexpectedly at one rehearsal and said:

"I am Wallace Greenslade, the Announcer."

"Of course you are," I said. "This is an act of sending you sideways, or up or down. You can go to the basement now."

"I am an ex-naval officer," said Wal, "and I feel I am on a craft heading on a collision course with disaster"

"Welcome dear Wal," I said. "Would you like a drink?"

"Yes."

"Well you had better go and get one.'"

'He was so ill-informed. He had been told he was going to read the nine o'clock news – so we let him. At nine o'clock we held up a card giving out gales in the Hebrides and riots in Bombay and then we continued with the show.'

Keeping the anarchic Goon Show on the rails was a major job for any of the BBC producers who worked on the show. As well as Pat Dixon and Peter Eton, Spike remembers working with a couple of others.

'Dennis Main-Wilson was a lunatic. He wanted to do ballet on the radio, you know. He later went on to the Marty Feldman Show. John Browell came in at the tail end of the Goon Shows. He observed the rules of the BBC. He always wore a collar and tie. He was a jolly decent chap and a very good front for the BBC. I have no idea how he looked from the back. They say there was no difference.'

All of the show's producers and the sound effects team had somehow to accomodate Spike's demanding requests for unusual sound effects, the style of which became a real trademark of the show.

'We created some marvellous sound effects, like the Wurlitzer organ crossing the Sahara Desert, changing key each time they change gear.'

And why did Spike spin the sound effects out longer than anyone else would have contemplated?

'Just daredevil, really.'

The Ray Ellington
Quartet in action for
television in 1959
(above) and Wallace
Greenslade in
jeopardy in 1955
(left).

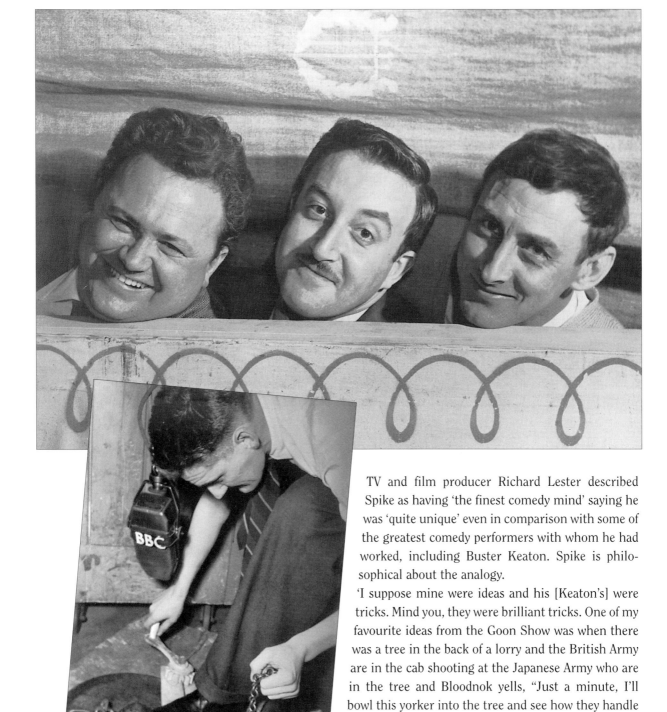

Sound effects man John P. Hamilton creating some eerie effects for The Goon Show using a ratchet and a length of chain.

TV and film producer Richard Lester described Spike as having 'the finest comedy mind' saying he was 'quite unique' even in comparison with some of the greatest comedy performers with whom he had worked, including Buster Keaton. Spike is philosophical about the analogy.

'I suppose mine were ideas and his [Keaton's] were tricks. Mind you, they were brilliant tricks. One of my favourite ideas from the Goon Show was when there was a tree in the back of a lorry and the British Army are in the cab shooting at the Japanese Army who are in the tree and Bloodnok yells, "Just a minute, I'll bowl this yorker into the tree and see how they handle it. Good heavens, they've surrendered!" They surrendered to a yorker. Let's see the Australians do that. I thought it was absolutely ridiculous, going along at 50 miles an hour and we bowl them out leg break.

'I don't remember any ideas which really went wrong. I suppose that puts me in the area of a perfectionist. I once invited the actor A.E. Matthews to come on the show. He was having an argument with the government about a lamp post being erected outside his cottage and he cocked it up completely. It wasn't funny and I remember the embarrassed laughter of the rest of the cast.'

Even at the height of the Goons' success, Spike doesn't recall ever really being aware of how famous they had become

'I couldn't believe it was such a success. It was like I was in some twilight

world. I had never been anything but a trumpet player. I just thought I was doing this show, I got paid for it and I went back to writing it every Monday. I was so certain of roars of laughter that I never doubted my ability to do it. Mind you, it had to be those characters saying the lines.

'In retrospect, I now realise that it was a breakthrough on a major scale in British humour, the like of which was very hard to follow. I stopped writing it because I thought that if I went on it would start to go downhill, and I wanted to leave it right at the top like a flat let by the Queen to elderly ladies at Hampton Court.

'Now most of those tapes lie gathering dust in the BBC. You'd think they would have the nouce to broadcast a series for a whole new generation of kids to hear it. Is there anybody listening?'

The Goons may have been a hard act to follow, but it spawned a number of new comedy shows including, of course, Monty Python. The Python team have always acknowledged Spike as the major influence on their style of humour and Spike recognised the echoes of his own work.

'I had already done that kind of thing in the Q series which, like the Goon Show, lies mouldering in the dust in the BBC cellars. I'm not surprised at the way the BBC eak out an occasional Goon Show recording rather than broadcast a whole series on radio, although I never expected it would still be going nearly fifty years later. The reason they can still distribute tapes, or now CDs, piecemeal is that it was the greatest comedy show ever. They don't repeat ITMA or Life With The Lyons or Ray's A Laugh. It's the quality of the Goon Show that gives them the ability to market it.

'I get a bit miffed about the slow pace of delivery of the Goon Show record-

Spike and Peter picking up their silver discs for achieving sales worth over £75,000 with 'The Last Goon Show Of All' LP. Harry was ill in bed with flu.

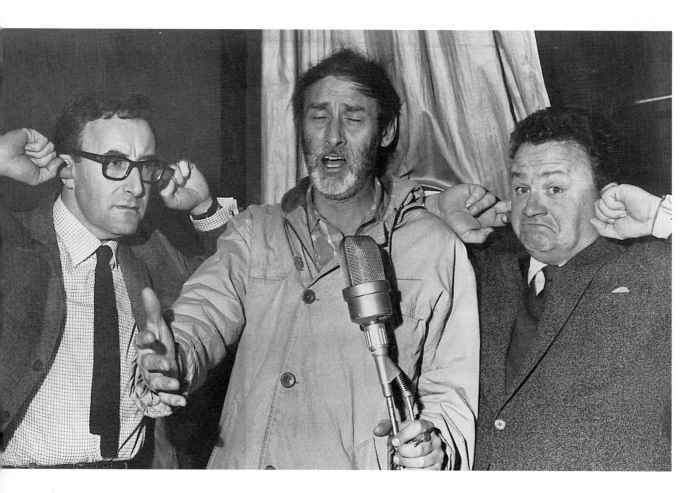

Three years after The Goon Show ended, they were back together again in a London Studio to record voices for The Telegoons.

ings. At this rate they will still be in the middle of Goon Show number 30 when I'm dead. They will outlive me.

'But wait . . . the money is very useful. I count it very carefully then spend it.'

By the time the televised Last Goon Show Of All was broadcast in 1972, it had been twelve years since the original radio series ended. Spike has fond memories of the old team getting back together again.

'It was like we had never been away. We had all changed. We had become more mature. Peter went into films; Harry went into prayers on Sunday and I tried to earn a living writing books.

'There was a certain euphoria about coming back after all that time. I really didn't want to do it, but the BBC had set it all up. I remember all the high-born people lounging in the bar. They made it impossible for us to say no. We were trapped. I don't even think it was a particularly funny script.

'One good thing, though, was that we invited the entire family and the children came along. Laura, Sean, Sile and Jane came up on to the stage when the audience were clapping and the applause was thunderous. I think that for the first time they knew what we were all about. I don't think they will ever forget that night.

'Did you know they would never let the Goon Show go out on the Light Programme? It always went out on the Home Service because they didn't think we could get the audiences. Silly them. Now a Goon Show is being eaked out for a miserable once-a-year airing on cassette. Blind, misguided, beaurocratic BBC.

'Despite all the continued adulation the BBC are ignoring the Goon Shows on radio and my Q series on television, so to the BBC, you are a lot of bastards, and here endeth the chapter.'

THE MYSTERY OF THE *MARIE CELESTE*
(solved)

The Goon Show: No. 107 (5th Series, No. 8)
Transmission: Tuesday 16 November 1954
8.30-9.00 p.m. Home Service. Studio: Paris Cinema, London

The main characters

Mr Henry Crun	Peter Sellers
Miss Minnie Bannister	Spike Milligan
Ned Seagoon	Harry Secombe
Admiral Grytpype-Thynne	Peter Sellers
Admiral Denis Bloodnok	Peter Sellers
Bloodnok's lady friend	Peter Sellers
Admiral Yakamoto	Spike Milligan
Eccles	Spike Milligan
Bluebottle	Peter Sellers
Old Sea Dog	Peter Sellers
Mr Snagge	Peter Sellers
Narrator	Peter Sellers

The Ray Ellington Quartet
Max Geldray
Orchestra Conducted by Wally Stott. Announcer: Wallace Greenslade
Script by Spike Milligan and Eric Sykes. Production by Peter Eton.

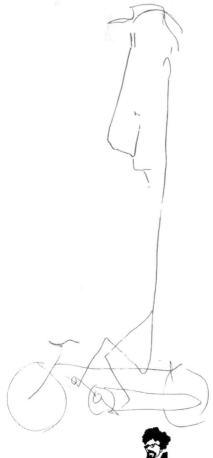

WAL	This is the BBC Home Service . . . OOH!
FX	Huge splashing sound as Greenslade is hurled into the water.
SEAGOON	Let that be a lesson to him. (sniggers) He was about to refer to the highly esteemed Goon Show!
ORCHESTRA	Cacophonous fanfare
SEAGOON	Listeners . . . what does that short, brief chord indicate? It indicates that Mr Wally Stott has forgotten the music again . . . and, therefore . . .
FX	Huge splashing sound as Wally Stott is hurled into the water
SEAGOON	. . . he'll be company for Mr Greenslade. Now then Mr Reserve Announcer . . .
SNAGGE	(heavy Jewish accent) What is it, nuts?
SEAGOON	Ah, Mr Snagge. Tell the British Empire and East Acton what we have decided is good for them. (sings) Let the joy bells ring . . .

SNAGGE	Muzzletoph. Ladies and Gentlemen. We 'ave been an' got a lot of geezers and spielers and we . . . OHH!!
FX	Huge splashing sound as Snagge is hurled into the water.
SEAGOON	Ladies and Gentlemen, on my own responsibility I present . . . The Mystery of The Marie Celeste – SOLVED!!!!
ORCHESTRA	Nautical high seas, tall-masted sailing ship-type theme.
NARRATOR	(heavy American accent) Unsolved in the nautical annals of sea mysteries is that of the brigantine Marie Celeste, but more of that later. Let us trace the thread of a rather unique experiment.
SPIKE	(Noel Coward voice) One spring afternoon in December, Ned Seagoon, a handsome young buck-about-town, decided to . . . dine out.
SEAGOON	Yes, as I sat in my usual place, I opened the Financial Times and carefully noted the number of chips I had left. I turned to the gossip page and helped myself to some fish. It was then that a small notice caught my eye. It read:

G-T	Author of sea stories will pay £5,000 to any person furnishing conclusive proof as to the fate of those who named the Marie Celeste.
SEAGOON	I read no further ...
G-T	But you don't know my address
SEAGOON	I read on.
G-T	Apply, Captain Grytpype-Thynne, First Mate, The Buildings, Hackney.
FX	Seagoon heading for Hackney at 2,000 mph followed by knocking on door.
G-T	Come in!
FX	Door knob turns, door opens.
SEAGOON	Captain Grytpype-Thynne?
G-T	Yes, matey?
SEAGOON	(aside) So this was the author of a thousand sea sagas. He was a tall, vile man dressed in the naval uniform of a sea-going

sailorr. Under his left arm he held a neatly rolled anchor, while with his right he scanned the horizon with a pair of powerful kippers.

G-T   Ahoy!

SEAGOON   Ahoy!

G-T   Ahoy! Pull up a bollard.

SAEGOON   Pardon?

G-T   That thing there is a bollard.

SEAGOON   Oh! Is that what you tie ships to?

G-T   Well said. Now, matey, what can I do for you?

SEAGOON   I have just read your offer in the paper about the Marie Celeste.

G-T   Little Matelot, that was inserted in 1910 – 44 years ago.

SEAGOON   My paper man has a big round.

G-T   Your paper man has a big round what?

SEAGOON   Ahoy!

G-T   Ahoy! Pull up a bollard. Little bosun, what do you know about the Marie Celeste?

SEAGOON   You're offering £5,000 for the mystery of it.

G-T   Hmmmm . . . do you come here often?

SEAGOON   No.

G-T   Good. Powder Monkey, let me tell you about the Marie Celeste. Ahoy!

SEAGOON   Ahoy!

G-T   Ahoy! At 3 o'clock on the afternoon of December 5th 1872, twixt the Azores and twixt the coast of Portugal, the Marie Celeste was sighted.

SEAGOON   Ahoy!

G-T   Ahoy! On board her there was no sign of life, and yet ...

SEAGOON   You're offering £5,000 reward?

G-T   Have you ever been shipwrecked?

SEAGOON   No.

G-T   I'll arrange for it.

SEAGOON   Ahoy!

G-T   Ahoy! Aboard the Marie Celeste all was ship-shape and Bristol fashion – food freshly laid, no sign of a struggle, and yet . . . and yet not a soul aboard her. Any questions?

SEAGOON   Yes. What's a bollard?

G-T   Ahoy!

SEAGOON   Thank you!

G-T   Yes, yes, yes. The crew disappeared without trace. Now, if you can furnish a satisfactory explanation as to what happened to them – £5,000.

SEAGOON   Right – I'm your man.

G-T   You silly, twisted boy, you.

SEAGOON   Give me a month and I'll have the answer by hook or by crook.

ORCHESTRA	Nautical, high seas, tall-masted etc. etc.
NARRATOR	And now ...
WAL	On the first stage of investigations, Ned Seagoon hurried round to the office of a large shipping magnate.
FX	Knock-knock-knock-knock
SEAGOON	Come in!
FX	Knock-knock-knock-knock
BLOODNOK	It's you that's knocking.
SEAGOON	Aha! Then I'll come in.
FX	Door knob turning, door opens.
SEAGOON	My name is Ned Seagoon.
BLOODNOK	I find no joy.
SEAGOON	Are you leading Admiral Dennis Bloodnok, chief of the International shipping line?
BLOODNOK	I have that privilege.
SEAGOON	I never knew there were shipping offices on the Serpentine.
BLOODNOK	Oh, yes, yes. I do all my business from here. What's the time?
SEAGOON	Quarter to five
BLOODNOK	Good heavens!
FX	Shuffle, footsteps, whistle.
BLOODNOK	Come in number 49!
FX	Shuffle, footsteps.
BLOODNOK	Now then, what can I do for you?
SEAGOON	Admiral Bloodnok, I wish to ...
BLOODNOK	Just a moment ...
FX	Shuffle, footsteps, whistle.
BLOODNOK	I shan't tell you again 49! Some of these people think I run these pleasure boats for pleasure. Now, lad, pull up a bollard.
SEAGOON	Admiral, I was told that you had associations with the ill-fated Marie Celeste.
BLOODNOK	All lies, d'you hear me, lies! I was in Bangalore at the time! I deny every word. She's lying, I tell you! Lying! And so is Alice Girth and Mary Thewler, and all the other women I mollested. They're all after my piggy bank, d'you hear me?

Grytpype - Thynne

SEAGOON	Admiral, please. Marie Celeste was found abandoned at sea.
BLOODNOK	Ohhh . . . poor girl! How she must have suffered.
SEAGOON	The Marie Celeste is a ship.
BLOODNOK	Of course! Wait a minute . . . of course! The Marie Celeste! I'd almost forgotten.
SEAGOON	Can you tell me anything about her?
BLOODNOK	Of course, I have the record here ...
SEAGOON	Ying-tong-yiddle-ay-po?
BLOODNOK	Good! Now, I'd like to tell you all about the Marie Celeste but unfortunately I'm sworn to secrecy, absolute mum. Yes, I'm afraid it would take a lot to make me talk.
SEAGOON	£5,000?
BLOODNOK	That's a lot. The entire documents are at your service.
SEAGOON	Thank you. (aside) For nights I pored over the vital documents and then, when all seemed lost, Admiral Bloodnok suddenly remembered a vital map reference.

BLOODNOK	Latitude 38° 29' north Longitude 17° 15' west. Off you go, lad!
SEAGOON	Right! Taxi! And now . . .
ORCHESTRA	Nautical tall-seas, high masted, etc.
BLOODNOK	I waited for Seagoon's return and then, at dawn ...
FX	Footsteps, door knob turning, door opens.
SEAGOON	Admiral, I have just returned from latitude 38° 29' north, longitude 17° 15' west.
BLOODNOK	You're soaking wet.
SEAGOON	You didn't tell me it was at sea!
BLOODNOK	Then it's true! The Marie Celeste was found at sea! Look, lad, here...
SEAGOON	Yes, yes, yes, yes, yes, yes, yes, yes, yes
BLOODNOK	Here, laddie. Here's the name of a shipyard, the very one that built her. Now, why don't you go along and see if they can give you any information?
SEAGOON	Aye-aye!
FX	Door knob turns, door opens and closes.
BLOODNOK	Aye-aye. (sings whilst dialling telephone) Sharing your gladness, my life's desire... Hello? Hello? Bloodnok here. Listen Mr Crun. What we planned for has happened. Yes. Ned Seagoon's the name. Yes. I've sent him to you and he's offering five...er...four thousand pounds reward for any information. Alright? Goodbye Mr Crun.
FX	Phone being hung up.
BLOODNOK	Seaman Geldray? Bring 49 in and play us a hornmouth on your pipe organ in the sea of key shanty...

CUE MAX GELDRAY MUSICAL INTERLUDE

WAL	'The Marie Celeste Mystery Solved. Part Two'. And now ...
ORCHESTRA	Nautical, sea-masted, high-tall, etc. etc.
SPIKE	While Max Geldray was playing that old English ballad, how many listeners noticed that Ned Seagoon had gone to a certain shipwright's in Deptford Creek . . . hmn? You must watch these points.
FX	Industrial clanking, banging and steam noises.
HENRY C.	(sings) Oooh, put him in the barrel until he's sober, put him in the barrel until he's sober, yin din din ...
MINNIE B.	(singing like a chicken) Yum-dum-da, yum-dum-diddle, yiddle-diddle-dadum-booo! Puddim on the bed-pan, lup cheerim, lak-yak-yak! Yim-bim-biddle-did-dle-diddle-da! Ha-hey!
HENRY	Minnie . . . stop that mad crazy modern rhythm-style singing.
MINNIE	Why should I stop my modern crazy rhythm . . . mnk ...mnk ...style singing . . . mnk . . . buddy?

Goon bird

HENRY	Mnk . . . because we are seafaring folk. If you must sing, sing a shanty.
MINNIE	(sings) Mmmm . . . aaah, it was only a shanty in . . . Yim-bim-biddle-diddle-diddle-die-biddle-diddle-yak-ya-yak-yee-yimmy-yak-yak! Wha-ha!
HENRY	Minnie!
MINNIE	Yeah?
HENRY	I shall come down there in a minute!
MINNIE	Baddle-biddle-hup-ha! Wha-ha!
HENRY	Shut up!
MINNIE	Wha-ha!
HENRY	(singing to Minnie's crazy rhythm) Rule Britannia, Britannia rules he waves! Breeeetons never never never shall be slaves.!
MINNIE	Baddle-biddle-burp-ah! Did-dee-dim-dee! Yik-dee-hum-ha-ha-ha!
HENRY	(singing more determinedly as the competition hots up) Fifteen men on a dead man's chest! Yo-ho-ho and a bottle of rum!
MINNIE	Ha-ha-hum-ha-hum ...
SEAGOON	Ahoy there!
HENRY	Ahoy!
SEAGOON	Ahoy! My name is Ned Seagoon.
HENRY	Oh, Minnie. It's him – Ned Seagoon.
MINNIE	Ya-ha . . .
HENRY	(sings over Minnie's rubbish) Rule Britannia, Britannia rules the waves! Breeeetons never never never shall be slaves!
SEAGOON	Thank you Anne Ziegler and Webster Booth. Is this the shipyard of Crun, Bannister and Crun?
HENRY	Yes.
MINNIE	Yes.

HENRY	And yes.
SEAGOON	Then, this firm built the Marie Celeste.
HENRY	Yes, I did.
SEAGOON	You did? Oh, come now. The Marie Celeste was built over a hundred years ago!
HENRY	Oh, then it must be my day off. Ahoy!
SEAGOON	Ahoy! Now, Mr Crun, I want you to build and man a second Marie Celeste.
HENRY & MINNIE	Ah . . . mnk . . . nyee . . . mnk . . .
SEAGOON	Don't you see?

The idea is to re-sail the ill-fated voyage and reconstruct the mystery.

HENRY	Build another Marie Celeste? Oh dear ...
SEAGGOON	Yes. I want you to build a replica.
HENRY	Oh, I'm sorry. I'm a ship builder. I'm no good at replicas.
MINNIE	Ying-tong-yiddle-ay-po.
ALL	Good!
SEAGOON	Now, how long to build it?
HENRY	Oh, well, there's a lot of work you know ...
MINNIE	Yes
HENRY	... a lot of work, isn't there Min?
MINNIE	There is, yes.
HENRY	The old plans will have to be modernised . . .
MINNIE	In the modern style, buddy.

Henry Crun

HENRY	Yes. Got to have the crazy plans, you know. Then there's the wood. It's very difficult to get the wood, you know. And the rope . . . ooh, the rope ...
SEAGOON	Yes, yes, yes. Now give me a rough date.
HENRY	. . . and deck timbers . . . and the canvas to go aloft . . .
SEAGOON	When will the boat be finished?
HENRY	Mmmm . . . after dinner.
SEAGOON	You'll have the whole ship completed after dinner?
HENRY	Yes
SEAGOON	What's the delay?
HENRY	The wood. You can't get the wood, you know.

SEAGOON	Alright, I'll just have to be patient. After dinner then. Ahoy!
HENRY	Ahoy!
SEAGOON	(Sings complete rubbish merrily.)
ORCHESTRA	Nautical-masted, sea-high, etc.
NARRATOR	And now ...
WAL	No sooner had young Ned Seagoon left the shipyard than Mr Crun hurriedly spoke to a seafaring man ...
HENRY	Commodore! Commodore! It's happened at last!
ECCLES	Wooooh! So it's happened at last eh? Well, well, well. So it's happened at last eh. Well. It's happened you say? It's happened.
HENRY	Yes, yes.
ECCLES	Wooh! Happened at last, eh? Yar, ow, what's happened?
HENRY	Admiral Bloodnok sent him to us and he's here.
ECCLES	Oooooh – wow – ooooh! Here? You mean he's really here? It's him?
HENRY	Yes, he's here.
ECCLES	He's here!
BOTH	(Manic jubilant laughter.)
ECCLES	Who's here?
HENRY	Him. Ned Seagoon. You know, the plan that we all worked on – the Marie Celeste plan.
ECCLES	Ooooh, dat one.
HENRY	Yes, and there's a reward for four . . . er . . . three thousand pounds.
ECCLES	Wooooh! Well I'll go and get the original crew.
HENRY	Yes, it's simple, all we have to do is to get . . . (fades out)
ORCHESTRA	Scene-changing roll of harp music.
CREW	Muted background conversation.
ECCLES	Listen, fellas, it's happened, fellas, it's happened and he's offering a reward of two thou . . . er . . . one thousand pounds!
OLD SEA	'Ere, d'you 'ear that, Seagoon 'n' Yakamoto? 'E's offerin' a reward DOG of one . . . er . . . five hundred pounds.
SEAGOON	What's he say?
YAKAMOTO	(heavy Japanese accent) Ah, Honourable man is offering five ...er ...two hundred and fifty pounds ...
SEAGOON	Is he? I'll tell cabin boy Bluebottle.

THE MYSTERY OF *THE MARIE CELESTE* (solved)

ORCHESTRA	Scene-changing roll of harp music.
B'BOTTLE	Eee-hi-hee! I have just been toll-ed there's a reward of seventeen and ninepence . . . and an extra bob a week – if we live.
SPIKE	Listeners, have you noticed a slight drop in the reward? You must watch these little points.
ORCHESTRA	Sea-masted, highly nautical, etc. (but faster)
NARRATOR	And now ...
WAL	Ned Seagoon hurried back to the author, who was offering four thousand pounds rewar ...
SEAGOON	Five thousand pounds!!!
WAL	I've got to live as well. Anyway, Ned Seagoon informed Admiral Grytpype-Thynne of the progress he had made and that he, Ned Seagoon, was preparing to re-sail the ill-fated voyage again.

SEAGOON	Correct! We sail today!
WAL	Now here is a gale warning.
SEAGOON	We sail tomorrow! We should reach the exact spot in five days.
BLOODNOK	In the meantime, Ray Ellington, pull up a bollard. Ahoy!
RAY	Ahoy!

CUE THE RAY ELLINGTON QUARTET

ORCHESTRA	Nautical highly-tall-sea, etc. (but even faster)
NARRATOR	And now ...
WAL	'The Mystery Of The Marie Celeste Solved – Part Three'. Exactly as in 1872, the brigantine Marie Celeste II slid gracefully out of harbour, past the boom and into the open sea . . .
FX	Seagulls, waves, etc.

SEAGOON	Well, we're underway, Cap'n.
BLOODNOK	Yes, yes. Put your hand out Seagoon. We turn left here, lad.
SEAGOON	(aside) Sometime later, I gave a last glance at land. It gave one a strange feeling to see the Beachy Head lighthouse pass our stern . . . we were at anchor. But soon, we were on the open sea ...
ORCHESTRA	Tall and naughty and very fast.
SEAGOON	After five days at sea, I was having dinner in the crow's nest when suddenly ...
ECCLES	Ahoy! You up dere Mr Seagoon?
SEAGOON	Yes!
ECCLES	Admiral Bloodnok's compliments, he wants you in his cabin straight away.
SEAGOON	Straight away.
ECCLES	Yeah . . . but first I want to tell you somethin'.
SEAGOON	Coming . . . WAAAAAAAAAA-AAAAAAAAAAAAA!
FX	Thuds as body hits deck.
SEAGOON	Ooch! Here, that's a nasty fall, that is.
ECCLES	Are you Okay?
SEAGOON	I think so – OOH! AAH! OOH! – Now, what did you want to tell me?
ECCLES	I've taken de ladder away.
HENRY	Mr Seagoon, we're nearly there. Then we can re-enact the mystery for you.
SEAGOON	Good. Wait a minute . . . do you know what happened to the original crew of the Marie Celeste?
HENRY	(sings) Mnyaaa . . . put him in the barrel . . . yum tum . . . (fades off)
SEAGOON	Mr Crun! Oh . . . I'll go and ask the Admiral. Perhaps he'll explain. Excuse me?
YAKAMOTO	Yah? What does honourable Neddie Sleagoon want?
SEAGOON	Where is Admiral Bloodnok's cabin?
YAKAMOTO	Tly the door there marked 'Ladies Only'.
SEAGOON	Thank you.
YAKAMOTO	Chip-chop-chap-chop
SEAGOON	Chop-chip. I strode towards the cabin, determined to get to the bottom of the mystery.

"ECCLES"

FX	Door chimes as on shop door as Seagoon opens door.
WOMAN	Yes?
SEAGOON	Oh, I'm terribly sorry. I thought this was the admiral's cabin.
WOMAN	Just one moment . . .
FX	Door closes.
BLOODNOK	Ahem! Come in.
FX	Door opens
SEAGOON	Admiral Bloodnok. You said you wanted to see me.
BLOODNOK	Oh, yes, yes, yes, yes, yes. Young Neddie, yes. You haven't met my sister have you?
SEAGOON	You told me you were an only child.
BLOODNOK	In that case, meet my mother.
SEAGOON	How do you do.
BLOODNOK	I'll see you later, mother dear.
WOMAN	Oh Dennis, Alright then. Ha-ha!
FX	Door closes.
SEAGOON	But, Admiral, you look twenty years older than she does.
BLOODNOK	Ah, yes, but I've had a lot of worry, you know. Now, Ned, to business. What about the . . . um . . . money?
SEAGOON	When we arrive at the rendezvous tomorrow, a naval vessel will be present with the author aboard.
BLOODNOK	Sir – I don't wish to know any author.
SEAGOON	He is the one with the money
BLOODNOK	Introduce me at once.
SEAGOON	He will not furnish the money until he receives a satisfactory explanation as to what happened to the crew . . .
BLOODNOK	Thud me marlin spikes. I know what happened. This is the true story. On the . . .
FX	Door knob turns, door opens
B'BOTTLE	Pardon me, my little hairy capitain . . . enter Bluebottle in rough seaman's itchy jersey and with a patch over one eye and a dirty big stocking on my head . . . Hurlay! Not a sausage ...
SEAGOON	Curse! Just as I was about to find the answer. What's going on here, little ragged pants?
B'BOTTLE	We have sighted a British man o'war, Haitch Hem Hess Gladys. Points with finger at the sea. We are getting ready to act de mystery. Stands by canyon to fire salute.

THE MYSTERY OF *THE MARIE CELESTE* (solved)

SEAGOON   What is the mystery of the Marie Celeste?

B'BOTTLE   Nay, nay! There is a seventeen and ninepence reward, and until I get it, not a word shall pass my lips. (Ties himself to mast and waits for fifty lashes.)

SEAGOON   Here's your seventeen shillings and ninepence. Now, out with it!

B'BOTTLE   Yee-hee-hee! Thank you. (Takes out seventeen and ninepenny piece which is no bigger than a tanner. Puts it in rough seaman's purse. Prepares to tell mystery.) Ahem . . . when we were ...eeeh! (Sees admiral out of the corner of eye.) Good job I've got square eyes.

FX   Bluebottle departs at 300 mph.

SEAGOON   I say little knobbly actor, I say . . . where's he gone?

BLOODNOK   Where's that naughty little powder monkey gone? It's time to fire a salute! Eccles!

ECCLES   Okay. Gimme the match. Stand back.

FX   Massive explosion, huge splash, pause –

B'BOTTLE   You rotten swine! Oh! I was hiding in the cannon. I'm drowning. Aiee! (Goes down for third time then remembers seventeen and ninepence in purse. Climbs back on ship to spend some. Exit left to NAFFI)

SEAGOON	Perhaps someone will tell me what's going on here?
BLOODNOK	I'll tell you. We are the original crew of the Marie Celeste.
SEAGOON	Good heavens! Ghosts!
ECCLES	We ain't ghosts.
SEAGOON	But you can't be human.
ECCLES	Oh, dat's different.
BLOODNOK	I'll . . . I'll tell you what happened. When we sailed the original Marie Celeste, we made rafts . . .
SEAGOON	Yes, yes, yes, yes, yes, yes, yes, yes, yes, yes...
BLOODNOK	Please don't do that! Then we set the table, left everything as it was. Then we quietly slipped over the side, and thud me gritkins that's really what happened. Isn't that right, me hearties?
ALL	Aye!
SEAGOON	But why did you do it?
BLOODNOK	Because we knew that one day someone would offer a reward for the solution of the mystery, and by thunder, it's happened! Hasn't it, me hearties?
ALL	Aye!
SEAGOON	But why couldn't you have just told me? Why come all this way?
BLOODNOK	They'd never believe us, lad. How some people can doubt me – me the very soul of honesty. Isn't that right, me hearties?
ALL	(silence)
CREWMAN	HMS Gladys on the port bow, sir!
SEAGOON	Splendid! On board is Captain Grytpype-Thynne with the £5,000!
BLOODNOK	Right. Stand by to re-enact the mystery, lads.
ECCLES	Okay, okay, okay, okay . . .
BLOODNOK	Ahoy, there, HMS Gladys! Captain Grytpype-Thynne. Are you ready with the money? That's funny . . . Ahoy there! HMS Gladys . . . !
FX	Sounds of lonely sea
ECCLES	HMS Gladys! Awohoyeee!
SEAGOON	Stand back, Eccles. Let me try. I used ot be in the choir. (high-pitched screeching voice) Ahoy there Captain Grytpype-Thynne!

Dennis Bloodnok

FX	Lonely sea sounds and long silence.
WAL	Here is the news. Two days ago a crew under the command of Admiral Bloodnok in the Marie Celeste II boarded a British sloop, HMS Gladys. On board all was ship-shape but there was no sign of life. Mr Neddie Seagoon is offering £5,000 reward for the solution of the mystery of HMS Gladys.
FX	Frantic knocking at door.
SEAGOON	Come in!
FX	Door knob turns, door opens.
G-T	Ahoy, there, matey.
SEAGOON	Ahoy.
G-T	About the reward money for the solution of HMS Gladys . . .
ORCHESTRA	Theme Tune
END	

HARRY SECOMBE'S STORY

The story of Harry Secombe's first meeting with Spike Milligan has been well documented elsewhere but, in essence, it happened in Italy during World War II when Gunner Milligan of the Royal Artillery came rushing down a hill in pursuit of a runaway field gun which had come thundering past Lance Bombardier Secombe's tent. Spike first appeared to Harry, therefore, in Eccles mode; a great lanky ill-dressed soldier yelling, 'Anybody seen a gun?'

'We did meet when the gun come over the cliff, and that's a well-known story, but I next met him when the Army formed something called the Central Pool of Artists at a place just outside Naples.'

The Central Pool of Artists was created in order to bring together entertainers who had found themselves in uniform fighting for King and country, and use them to put on shows for the entertainment of their comrades.

'I arrived at this sort of barrack room, having come up from the Royal Artillery Training Depot where I had been doing concerts. I had been invalided and downgraded after I got lost in a blizzard. I'd been performing in concerts and arrived along with this fellow called Bill Hall, who had been with me in the same sort

Left: Not the wild west but Southend as Spike and Harry square up for a TV special in 1955.

Below: Harry (left) serving King and country.

of concert party. He was a fantastic fiddle player.

'Spike turned up with his trumpet and guitar and I took to him straight away. Spike and me and Bill chatted for a while and then a bloke called Johnny Mulgrew brought out this bass . . . strange, because you don't normally find someone walking around with a double bass. He and Spike and Bill Hall began playing and it was a fabulous moment, completely impromptu.

'They became the Bill Hall Trio and appeared in a show called Over The Page where I was the principal comic. I got on like a house on fire with Spike because we shared the same type of humour. We'd both been through the mill as soldiers and a bond forms between you under those sorts of conditions which you can't really explain to other people. It's beyond the scope of normal experience. You know, I still go to all the regimental reunions, and I think Spike tries to as well, because you forge bonds with those fellows that never break.

'It's very difficult to explain to people, even my own kids, what war is really like - what it's like to be shot at. It's the noise and the smell and all the rest of it. It anaesthetises folk

'We shared the same sense of humour, a kind of madness we had, but it wasn't always appreciated by Spike. I remember we were in a hostel in Rome when

The Bill Hall Trio dressed in their trademark stage rags.

we were doing Over The Page. We did anything for a gag. Everybody bunked down together, sleeping on the floor - sleeping anywhere, in fact - and it was pyjama time. I came in and there was Spike all tucked up in bed, nice and comfortable with his pyjamas on . . . so I poured a bottle of beer over his head. He chased me out of the room. He was very upset. Everyone else had a laugh and he did too - eventually. So he qualified - anything for a gag. There was an affinity between us then that has never been broken as far as I am concerned.'

Harry was already making a meagre living as a performer back home in England when Spike eventually returned from Italy and he played a part in bringing together the rest of the embryonic Goons.

'I was a sort of catalyst in that way, I suppose. By the time Spike came back - he had stayed on in Italy with the Bill Hall Trio after they were demobbed - I had fixed up a gig for them in the Coconut Grove or the Blue Lagoon or some other grotty club I had been playing. I forget the bloke who used to book us, but I put them in touch and they got a job playing in the cabaret.

'I was auditioned for the Windmill Theatre in August 1946. Norman Wisdom was at the same audition. He came on, told a joke, fell down - "Thank you," said Van Dam [the owner] and he went off. That was his lot. I got the job.

'The show that followed the one I was in at the Windmill featured a duo called Sherwood and Forest. It was a very funny act. One bloke played the piano and the other played the drums. Tony Sherwood was the pianist and Mike Bentine was Mike Forest. I dashed on to speak to them after the dress rehearsal and it was obvious that we were on the same kick. We became very friendly and

Rehearsing in the
Grafton Arms in 1951
for The Crazy People.

An early Goons publicity shot.

he took me down to Jimmy Grafton's pub, telling me that he knew a place where we could get drinks after hours - WAHAAAY - not a bad idea.'

Ex-Major Grafton was, of course, hugely sympathetic towards demobbed strays who were trying to make their way in showbusiness and, in or out of hours, Harry and Michael soon became regulars at the Grafton Arms. Harry also began to pick up work as a comedian on radio.

'Jimmy ran the pub along with his twin brother - you couldn't tell them apart - but he was also scriptwriting for Derek Roy. The pub became a sort of a base. Then I met up again with Spike, introduced Spike to Mike at the pub and later Peter came along.

'By that time I was doing things for Pat Dixon, this wonderful BBC producer who had a great eye for talent. He was always looking for new people and he was a great picker. He produced shows like Third Division and Listen My children, programmes that went out on the BBC Home Service with performers like Benny Hill, Vic Lewis and Bob Beatty. It was all very clever stuff, very advanced humour written by Frank Muir and Denis Norden. Everything was exciting about it.

'Pat also found lots of singers who were later used by Peter Sellers in 'Songs For Swinging Sellers' – 'Balham Gateway To The South' was one of them. We were also all mucking around with different voices. I used to mess around with an old Grundig wire recorder, too. Eventually Spike, Michael, Peter and I started meeting up in the back room at old Jimmy Grafton's place and he declared it KOGVOS – King Of Goon Voices Society.'

Harry's is just one interpetation of KOGVOS. The acronym has also been described as a conjugation of King Of Goons and Voice Of Sanity or Keeper Of Goons and Voice Of Sanity, both in reference to Jimmy Grafton. In any case, there is no doubt that the Grafton Arms was the birthplace of the Goons. The four Goons were, in fact, becoming quite inseparable.

'Spike and I shared a flat for a while in Linden Gardens, Notting Hill Gate in London. There were only supposed to be two people staying in this place, but we managed to get three in. I used to sleep on the floor. Spike and Michael Bentine had the beds. Spike was obsessively tidy in those days and he was always complaining about my socks. Those were happy days.'

The showbusiness community has always been a fairly tight-knit brotherhood, especially for comedians, and Harry recalls many of the other performers whom he came to know.

'Norman Vaughan had come out of the army at the same time as us. He had also been in the Central Pool of Artists. Alfred Marx was around at the time and Jimmy Edwards and Muir and Norden, too. We all used to meet up in Daddy Allen's Club in Windmill Street. There was a great affinity between us all. We were like tadpoles in a great big pond.

'When we were appearing at the Windmill Theatre, Daddy Allen's was the place we'd meet. Even long after you'd left the Windmill, you could eat on the slate and pay later - eating on tick. He was great, old Daddy Allen, and so many people used to go to this little drinking club. It was a nucleus of new comedy. They were exciting times, they really were.'

When the Photo Fair exhibition opened at London's Olympia in May 1959, Harry was there to lend a hand.

Above: Harry with Alfred Marx at rehearsals for Marx's 1956 TV show Comedy Hour.

Below: Dick Bentley, Frank Muir and Denis Norden discuss a script circa 1950.

Harry was enjoying increasing success as a solo artist but his energy and boundless enthusiasm made him an indispensable member of the Goons. He was certainly proud to be part of the team.

'The only way to get on in those days was in variety . . . and then on radio. Radio was the place to be. I was a solo act from the beginning, only getting together with the Goons on Sunday, but I was so happy to be in that camp. We all sparked off each other and there was so much energy it could have powered the Queen Mary.

'It was with Spike and Mike where there could be a bit of conflict. They would both have lots of ideas when we were sitting around chatting. Mike would throw off ideas like sparks from a Catherine wheel and Spike would pick up on them and then it would be back to Michael. In the end they would both go away, each thinking that the idea was his. Silly really, because then there would be the odd argument.

'Mike, of course, represented everything Spike wasn't. Mike was an old Etonian and he had been an officer. Spike and I were non-commissioned – a

lance bombardier and a lance sergeant. I was a bit in awe of Bentine because of his tremendous intellectual capacity. I mean, he had been to Eton and I had been to a Welsh secondary school. He used to talk about dorm feasts and pranks. As far as I was concerned prank was Chinese for a piece of wood!

'Spike, of course was educated partly in India in a convent school. He had this tremendous imagery, but wasn't always able to spell out what he wanted. He had a wonderful gift for surreal humour which I think we understood and joined in. It wouldn't have been any good for us to have had someone like Max Miller with us. He wouldn't have understood what we were all about. We were different. We had things in commom such as a liking for Edward Lear or Lewis Carroll. There was a chemistry there between the four of us that happens very rarely.'

The chemistry which created such a vital element of the Goon Show could not be turned on and off at will. It was at work whenever the four were together, even, as Harry remembers, at the cinema.

'We would go to the news cinemas and often see something completely mad. The news shows would run for about an hour and there was one that we sat through three times. It included a movietone news item about a great white shark in Australia. They had caught this massive shark and propped the jaws open with a stick. It really was a frightening ceature. Then somebody pulled the stick away and the jaws collapsed with a GLUMP! Suddenly this ferocious creature had been turned into an idiot. We sat through this three times and were then thrown out for laughing.'

Publicity shot of Harry from 1957.

The Goon Show became more and more popular just as Harry's own career was going from strength to strength. He always looked forward to his Sunday with the Goons, relaxing into the routine, although he admits that it was totally different for Spike.

'The Goon Show was a bit of fun on Sunday, to be honest. Peter and Mike and myself went off and did our own individual things. I would be in the theatre and

Harry shows off his physique during a break in rehearsals for the 1957 TV show Saturday Spectacular.

so would Mike. Peter, of course, was into films but the one thing we lived for was to get together on Sundays and then the rest of the week just blew away.

'It's a tribute to Spike that he went on creating to such a wonderful standard all the time, while we were swanning along doing our own individual bits, earning lots of money and capitalising on our radio fame. Spike, poor bugger, had to sit there writing. It wrecked his health and his first marriage. He is the one who suffered and I can understand why he has always been reluctant to talk about the Goons. I think that represented a very traumatic part of his life.

Clowning with Peter and Spike during a Goon Show recording.

'On the other hand, we could never wait to see the script. We just read it and fell about laughing at it. We would do a run-through with the band and that was it. We didn't have to be there until four o'clock in the afternoon. On some of those Sundays I was doing Educating Archie as well. I would do one show, then run between studios for the next. At one time, Dennis Main Wilson called me in when he had a panic on with Hancock's Half Hour and I did that for three weeks. So I was then doing three radio shows on the same Sunday but it was a fun thing to do. If I was in variety I would drive down from as far away as Glasgow to do the show – and to go to my singing lesson at 11 o'clock.

'I had twelve years of singing lessons with old Manlio di Veroli. He taught me how to sing opera. I used to fit that in before the Goons. Manlio di Veroli was one of the Italian maestros. He was a freind of Gigli. I met Gigli with him on several occasions in this little studio he had in Marble Arch. You climbed up the stairs and there was a gorgeous smell of Italian cooking. His wife used to make marvellous spaghetti. I used to be drooling as I did my scales. He taught me how to produce a voice. It was probably the secret of that terrible ring about Neddy's "Hello", and why when they asked me to do any other voice it always sounded like me anway!'

Given the closeness of the four, and later three, Goons, Harry bears a sneaking admiration for those at the BBC whose job it was to try to keep them in line.

'The producer who was best was Peter Eton. He was a disciplinarian and he didn't care if we kicked up a fuss - he sorted us out. He was great. He used to get quite choleric, go all red and shout, "You bastards sit down!" Peter Sellers would say, "I'm pissing off" and Eton would just say, "Well, go then!"

'If more of that had happened to Spike and the rest of us earlier on we would have been . . . not as funny perhaps? Before Peter Eton the show was a series of sketches which didn't have any chronological sequence and we all spoke so quickly it was a gabble. Peter Eton was a drama producer and he brought his drama experience to play in the Goon Shows. Spike readily fell in with that.'

Peter Eton was, perhaps, able to make happen what Spike, in discussion with Eric Sykes, already had in mind for the show but there were others whose contributions Harry is keen to acknowledge.

'Pat Dixon was the one who really saw it in the beginning. Jimmy Grafton and Spike took the idea for the show to him and we made a pilot which the BBC, in its infinite wisdom, took up. It was Pat Dixon's foresight which really brought it all together. I don't think Jimmy Grafton has ever really been given enough recognition for his part in the Goons. He really helped a hell of

Harry holds up Valentine Dyall with a new-fangled loudhailer whilst filming a TV commercial in 1956.

a lot. Spike used to live in his loft, you know. We used to call him the Prisoner of Zenda.

'Jimmy was a bit more pedantic than the rest of us and saw things in a different way, perhaps. He tightened things up. We were so diffuse and he would narrow things down. I think Spike sometimes resented that in some ways. Jimmy fostered the Goons but you have to admit that the driving force behind it all was Spike. He was the one who had the ideas; the one who had the imagery. We were once referred to as riding on the thermal currents of his imagination. Only when Michael Bentine left did it really begin - really take shape.

'Mike went off because he was more focused on what he wanted to do, which was fair enough. Spike was always more wide ranging in his madness. Gradually Mike's departure did make a difference. Before, when there were four of us, it was a bit of a shambles in some respects. Spike and Michael would fight over certain things, not stand-up rows, but there was sometimes a really uneasy situation.

Harry and Beryl Reid as Perce and Marlene in ATV's Sunday Night At The London Palladium, 1956.

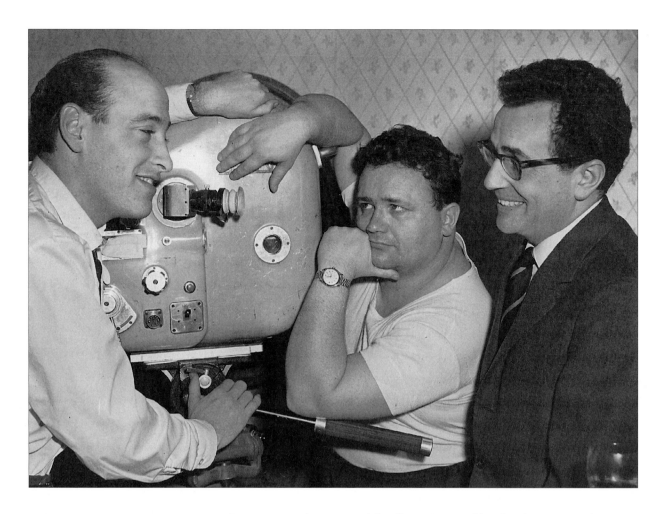

Dick Lester filming an interview with Harry and Michael Bentine.

'I was never privy to any of the discussions and battles that went on between Spike and the BBC because I would be off doing something at the Windmill or somewhere. I only saw the tail end of such things when we all got together on the Sunday. Peter Eton would sometimes phone me on a Saturday night, though, and say, "Get in early tomorrow because Spike and Peter have had a row." We were all living in the same block of flats, so I would go down there to sort them out - I was a big lad in those days - "Just a minute lads!!!"'

Although Harry always knew that the Goon Show was something very special, he didn't realise the effect it was having on the general populace until he started to hear echoes of the show on the streets.

'Spike would make up something like "ying tong yiddle I poo" and you would go out in the street and hear somebody saying it. That was the part of it all that I found frightening. That kind of power is frightening, but it was very exciting. By the time the show became a sort of cult, people used to fight to get in there, fight to get tickets for the recording at the Camden Theatre. This created an urgency about it and there was a great desire to do new things. As we got more used to working together, Spike became more experimental. He is a perfectionist and always wanted to try to get exactly the right sound effects.

'We never saw the script in advance. We would see it at four o'clock on the Sunday afternoon when we sat down for the first read-through. Spike would be watching us like a hawk to see where the laughs came and when they did come he was always so relieved!'

Appearing on stage and on radio as often as he was, Harry saw and heard all of the top comedy performers of the day. The Goon Show was always decidedly

different, but there were other acts which also made him laugh.

'At the time I admired Ted Ray's sharpness and Jimmy Edwards was a good mate of mine. I liked Jimmy. I was topping the bill at the Palladium for a few years. I did five shows in ten years from 1956 to 1966 so all of the top comedians were my contemporaries. Tommy Cooper made me laugh. Hancock I knew very well - he was a tortured soul - and there was no more morose individual than Frankie Howerd. They were all different. That was the thing about all of us who came out of the services. We were all different. Max Bygraves and

'. . . Spike would be watching us like a hawk to see where the laughs came . . .'

All that clowning around has to go wrong sometime, and in 1956, Harry broke his arm.

Norman Wisdom were completely different, too.

'I wasn't that enamoured of the savage comedians of the day. I felt it was our job to chop them down. I admired people like Red Skelton. I think that most comics begin as impressionists and eventually you become an amalgam of all the best of everyone else and that's how you're remembered. That's the only kind of immortality a comedian can have. You can't save a round of applause. You can't put a standing ovation on a mantlepiece.

'I'm not at all happy about the way comedy is going now because a lot of it is so cruel – and it's crude. We used the pay-offs to naughty army jokes, but not the joke itself, so it was up to you to laugh if you wanted to. We didn't corrupt, we tried to inspire and again it's a tribute to Spike that the Goons is seen as a watershed in comedy. The Python lads gladly recognise that and say so quite often, so we were an influence.

'I think that the special thing that we had came from being all men together who had been through the services where you had to provide your own

entertainment. We did things to make each other laugh. We didn't really have radio or anything like that. Then, just as the the servicemen's vote got Churchill out because they thought he'd done his job and it was time for a change, the same thing applied to comedy. We got rid of established comedy because we thought, enough is enough, they've become fat cats while we've been in the army, so out you go, lads.'

Now, half a century on from the early days in the Grafton Arms, the enduring popularity of the Goon Show recordings comes as no real surprise to Harry.

'What Spike created is very rare. It is his genius that has made the Goon Show last. It doesn't date and kids today whose fathers weren't even born when the Goon Show finished are being brought up in the Goon tradition with all the tapes.

'It wasn't topical. Nothing dates more than topical humour. Just listen to Ray's A Laugh or ITMA. They are very dated. Spike didn't do that. The Goon voices were funny, too, but these voices were based on real people. Sellers based

Despite the manic energy he exuded, Harry was seen as the most stable one of the three.

a character on somebody he had met – like Bluebottle, the man who came to us and told us "Michael Bentine said I'm a genius!" There was another voice Peter based on a second-hand-car salesman. There was a wonderful combination of Seller's capacity for creating voices and Spike's capacity for writing great material. I suppose I was the comic straight man.

'The greatest tribute you can pay to Spike's genius is that the Goon Shows read funnily. A lot of radio stuff relied on funny voices. We did funny voices, but we had funny scripts to do and that was the magical thing. Eric Sykes wrote some very funny Goon Shows, too. The Lurgi one, that was one of Eric's. Of course, we mustn't forget Larry Stephens' part in it. He wrote with Spike in the beginning. He was an ex-officer, too. So there were the two of us - Spike and me, hairy-arsed devils – and three officers if you included Jimmy Grafton. I think that part of the chip on Spike's shoulder was this anti-officer thing. When he was brought up in India as a warrant officer's son, he wasn't allowed to play with the officers' children and I think it must have rankled.'

Harry looks back on some golden memories from the Goon Show years which he rekindles occasionally by replaying some of the shows, and if he had the chance to do it all again, he wouldn't change a thing.

'I still listen to the shows now and then, not so much for the content,

In 1959 Harry was struck down with, not the plin or the nadgers, but the mumps.

Opposite: In 1958, Harry starred in his first feature film, Davy, a comedy about a family music hall act.

Harry is the centre of attention at the Grafton Arms where Jimmy Grafton plays host to, amongst others, Michael Bentine, Eamon Andrews, Beryl Reid, Dickie Henderson and Eric Sykes.

because I remember the stories, but I listen to the background and the little giggles we had between us – unmentionable things, really – little hysterical chuckles at the back. I remember the warm-ups, too, because we could really let ourselves go there.

'I've been very lucky. I'm always expecting a tap on the shoulder and a voice saying, "All right, let's have it all back. Keys to the house, the lot." You could have it all gladly because I've had a great time. I've been very happy, very lucky in my married life with four lovely kids, a smashing wife and five grandchildren. I had a very serious illness a few years ago and you do a sort of reappraisal of your life once you have felt what they call the brush of angels' wings. You say, "Hello, folks. What are we all stampeding towards?" You begin to think about what you have got and it becomes more precious to you.

'I became invloved in a lot of religious programmes after that. Not as a guru – I think that's the worst thing in the world. When I've done these programmes, I've always tried to ask the questions the viewers want an answer to rather than being somebody holier than thou. I try to steer away from that.

'I think that I can say that my life has been enriched by the Goon Show. It taught me a lot. It taught me tolerance, the way the original four got on together, then the companionship of the three of us and then there was Spike. I'll always regard him as a very close friend.

'I think Spike would like to be remembered for his poetry and his writing, but he's going to be known for the Goons. We all are. Sellers at the height of his fame was always "ex-Goon" or "arch-Goon". It's a label we should accept gladly.'

Harry at a costume fitting for the stage show The Four Musketeers in 1967.

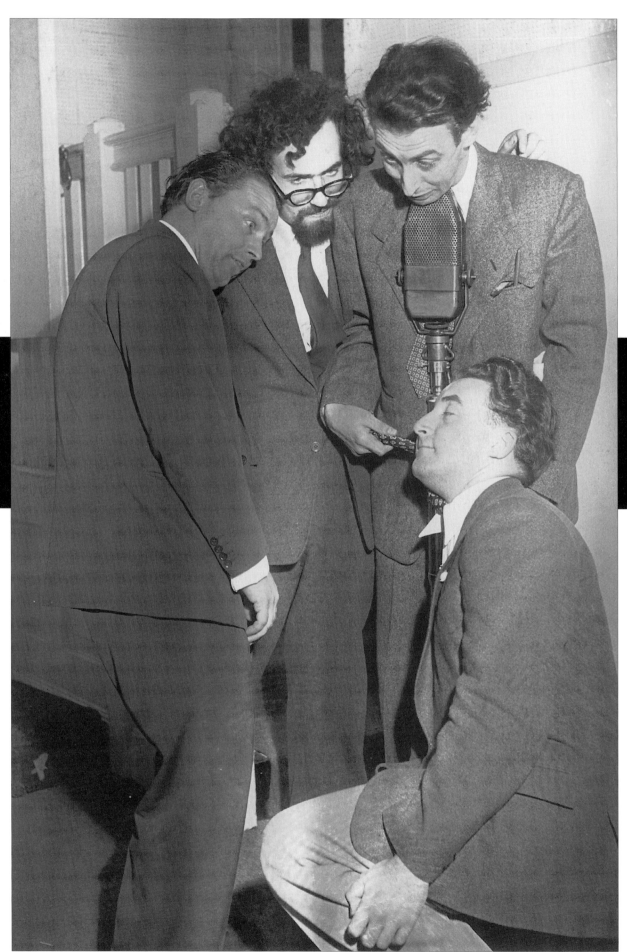

THE GOONS The Story – part 2

For the second pilot, too, another producer was assigned to the, ultimately successful, project. As far as the young Dennis Main Wilson was concerned, his becoming involved in the project was the result of 'a senior producer being very kind to a promising junior. . . Mind you, [Pat] could see the kind of trouble that was coming!' It was one thing for an ambitious group of young comics to produce a convincing pilot, quite another to sustain the ideas and cope with the pressures involved in the week-after-week grind of a series that could run for up to 26 weeks of the year. Any producer embarking upon such a project was not going to have an easy time of it.

The BBC and the Goons clashed almost from the moment the project was commissioned. What was the show to be called? The Goon Show seemed a quite meaningless title to the planners (about which Spike observed, quite fairly, 'so who are Take It From Here then?'). Their alternative title The Junior Crazy Gang, was just as unacceptable to the Goons, since the style and humour of the Crazy Gang was precisely the kind of thing against which they were reacting. In the end a compromise title of Crazy People was used for the first series of programmes (even this was of course relentlessly subverted by the Goons until the BBC eventually gave in and allowed then to call it The Goon Show).

Crazy People was first broadcast on 28 May 1951. It appeared as a programme in the standard Variety format of that time, a series of freestanding sketches and three or four musical items. The Ray Ellington Quartet provided arrangements of popular melodies, mostly as a vehicle for Ray himself to sing.

Ray Ellington, leader of the
Ray Ellington Quartet.

Max Geldray provided a virtuoso harmonica instrumental spot, whilst the third spot went to The Stargazers, a close harmony singing group. Harry would provide a fourth musical item, usually of a light operatic nature.

The early Goon routines were to some extent personality-led and the key performer would be introduced by name before launching full bloodedly into his sketch, with the other Goons taking a supporting characterisation. As a result of this device, common enough at the time in radio, there was rarely any continuity between sketches through an entire show.

By far the most distinctive voice in the early shows was Michael Bentine's Professor Osric Pureheart. Pureheart's activities more often than not featured something based around a scientific or engineering feat, such as the building of the Crystal Palace, the Suez Canal, the designing of Jet Fighter X9 or a new lead violin for deaf people. His designs would suffer from some fatal flaw (after all, why bother to insure an enormous glass Palace against fire? Silly idea) or be overcome by the actions of lesser beings who would ruin his beautifully dug Canal by filling it with water.

Harry's earliest scenes seem to be either as Handsome Harry on some heroic task (thereby anticipating that final metamorphosis of himself into British patriotic hero and twit Neddie Seagoon later in the Goon saga) or as part of the character team Herschell and Jones. Peter would often refer to Harry as 'Hersch' in conversation for many many years thereafter, long after the character had faded from popular recall (or even Harry's!).

The first producer, Dennis Main Wilson.

The exploits of Major Denis Bloodnok heralded a performance from Peter from quite early in the genealogy of The Goon Shows, although this Bloodnok was less haunted by curry addiction and financial embarrassment to begin with. Moreover, each of these 'set piece' routines would be heralded, in manner typical of the time, by a signature tune. The only signature tune to survive The Goon Show's gradual metamorphosis into the entity known today is the theme for Bloodnok (though the later version was usually followed by some explosive catastrophe for the Major), used even on The Last Goon Show of All.

At those beginning times of the first few series of Shows, the only Goon to whom a routine was not dedicated was Spike himself, strange as it may seem in retrospect. The fact of the matter, readily admitted by Milligan himself, was that it took a while for his confidence as a performer to build, by which time the format of the Show had changed considerably. 'I wasn't performing much at the beginning. I used to say "Yes" and "Shut the window" and do odd voices. I didn't think I could compete with Harry and Peter. I was frightened. They all had good egos and they were young. I was always in their lee as a performer, and I never reversed that until I did Oblomov. . .'

Very little recorded evidence has survived of the earliest Goon Shows. Even in the first series, they attracted enough listeners for the BBC to repeat the

Shows on Saturday mornings from about 4 August 1951. Such scratchy excerpts still testify to lots of energy, great enthusiasm and a huge supply of ideas – to produce four or five viable sketches for transmission on radio each week hints at many more that didn't quite make it. In this respect the enthusiasm which was such a profound hallmark of Dennis Main Wilson's production style had a great store of electric creativity to work on.

Electricity, however, has to be handled carefully. Two of the biggest contributors of raw ideas to the early scripts among the Goons were, of course, Michael and Spike. It was subsequently observed by Peter Eton that Michael was quite lively in brainstorming sessions. '[He] used to come to rehearsals with many ideas that were in the Goon area, but they were often visual, always clever, and the characters were very funny. Mike was a noisy person, always ("Look, hey, I've got a marvellous idea!") and Spike is very quiet. . .'

Sellers remembered the energy of that process vividly. 'We were brimming over with ideas – we had sessions where we sat around – building mad, lightning sketches . . .'

Dennis Main Wilson also recalled those times and identified subtle differences in the thought processes of Messrs. Milligan and Bentine. 'If you were to analyse the difference between Michael and Spike, it is the difference between being organic and inorganic. Michael was the technical creator of documentary items, in terms of humour, but they had no heart and no soul in them. Whereas Spike had great heart, great soul and great imagination but he wasn't that good at technique . . . yet." While such differing strengths could complement each other, difficulties could arise if one or other sought to dominate the ideas process.

In the meantime matters went on apace. After seventeen shows, the first series ended and the only other Goon production in that year was a Christmas pantomime entitled Goonderella ('Surrealism and crumpet', remarked Main Wilson). It also featured as 'Prince Charming' a supporting actor who was later involved in several Goon-type projects, Graham Stark.

Subtle changes came with the start of the second series of Shows in 1952. For one thing, a series of carefully staged BBC photos showed the trials and tribulations of Dennis as he 'tried' to get the Goons to sign up for that second series. They also heralded the final success of the team as being announced in Radio Times as The Goon Show (featuring those Crazy People . . .).

Another change soon after the series began was the leaving of The Stargazers. Four musical items within the space of a half-hour Show did tend to swamp the comedy. Moreover, although this was not the rationale at the time and not obvious until much later, The Goon Show was also freed from a style of music which was clearly of the Fifties and would have enabled future listeners to 'pigeonhole' The Goon Show far more easily. With Max Geldray and Ray Ellington playing what Harry called 'the evergreen melodies', music complemented the character of the comedy so that the entire programme became far more timeless.

Nevertheless, the same pattern was kept, with four or three sketches per Show. More established characterisation appeared in the 'set piece' sketches though they remained personality-led, with more lunatic escapades such as Pureheart and Dick Barton's Interplanetary Adventures, or Von Bloodnok – German Secret Agent or even Handsome Harry – On Trial for Singing (!) and a demonstration of the power of gravity.

Harry: Would any gentleman care to come on stage. Ah, you sir, thank you.

Eccles: Da. That's OK.

Harry: Now jump into the air.

Eccles: OK

FX (jump..... pause..... down)

Harry: Now you see what happened, you jumped into the air, but you came back to earth, - now, why?

Eccles: Da... Cos I live dere.

A run of 25 Shows this time, with the sustaining and development of more than 70 Goonish ideas onto the air, did not solve the underlying creative tensions. However, Michael Bentine's decision not to continue with The Goon Show at the end of that series did. He wished to have more time with his family, something hard to come by when all the programme recordings for The Goon Show were done on a Sunday. The strengths of his brand of comedy, identified by Dennis Main Wilson, were seen in his subsequent comedy projects but would not have harmonised with the great moments which were to come on The Goon Show.

Michael puts the point of his leaving like this. 'I was always a breakaway Goon with an urge to apply my logical nonsense as opposed to their nonsensical logic . . . I was with The Goon Show until 1952, so the six years from 1946 represent a large chunk of my life. I remember we suffered enormous tensions in putting the shows together, but there was also the joyous side and the memories all four of us have. My relationship with Harry, Peter and Spike, which developed over those years, is an intensely personal one, and we found a friendship that is for ever . . ." Michael and Spike have indeed met quite happily and

Top: Peter Sellers remonstrates while Spike Milligan looks on.

Above: Spike in more thoughtful mood.

Far left: Michael Bentine takes the plunge while Harry Secombe purses his lips at the prospect.

Michael Bentine and Peter Sellers with writer David Nettheim.

Max Geldray at the microphone.

talked on the same platform about comedy and The Goon Show in the years since the Show finally ended.

Dennis Main Wilson was also lost to the Show at the end of that series. His producing career was already beginning to expand with other projects being accepted by the BBC planners and he went on in a relatively short space of time to produce Tony Hancock in Hancock's Half Hour. There were other aspects to the decision, however. Main Wilson was mindful of the pent-up energy in those four Goons working together, when he recalled that 'Spike confided in me once, "What I need, Den, is a strong producer." Well, I'd played that game before, and it wasn't going to be me!'

The person that it was going to be, Main Wilson recalled with relish, was a hard man to make laugh, who he had affectionately nicknamed "The Pirate" because of a limp earned during active service in the Navy.

Peter Eton produced The Goon Show for the next three years and imparted all the strength in production that Milligan could possibly have wanted, if not more. '[Spike] was . . . never robust. If I knew he wasn't very well, I used to exert more influence . . . I did used to have rather a bad temper, and if it was a bad day for me I'd bully and get what I wanted...' Eton's background was in drama, not comedy and this enabled him to bring onto the Show a demand for

Top: Fondly remembering the good times.
Above: Michael Bentine in a scene from his own series, Bentine.

The Goons remained good friends after the series ended.

Peter Eton (centre) became producer after the departure of Dennis Main Wilson.

structure from which some of Spike's more way-out ideas benefited.

Eton caused the character of the programme to change considerably. It can be heard in the earliest surviving recordings from his time on the Show although these do not include (to the continuing angst of fans everywhere) any examples whatsoever of that third series of The Goon Show recorded during 1953.

(A major reason for the loss of Series Three recordings was a rationalisation by the BBC in 1962 of their comedy recording holdings, after the series finally came off the air. Decisions were made that attempted to preserve a selection which was representative of the style and range of the Show during its run of nine years. However, there was no attempt to retain any of the earliest recordings from disc. The preferred medium to work from was magnetic tape originated recordings, as much as anything else because there were many of the latter easily accessible and of better quality at source. One direct result of this decision was the loss of virtually all The Goon Shows featuring Michael Bentine to posterity [as well as Series Three]. This decision was made by the BBC purely for practical technical reasons and not with specific intent to eliminate Michael's contribution from Goon history).

The surviving written evidence shows how Eton changed the structure of the programme even more. Only two musical breaks were permitted now, Ray and Max performing one musical item each (perhaps that prosecution of Handsome Harry for singing had something to do with it). More time was freed for the comedy of the Shows and the development of comic ideas.

The early part of this series was also marked, however, by one of the darker aspects of the story of The Goon Show – the first hospitalisation of Spike Milligan with a nervous breakdown from overwork.

The warning signs for this went back into the pressure of writing on the previous two series. Friends who saw him at the time, apart from the Goons, during 1952 commented that '[Spike] always had that haunted, weary look and a tension about him . . . He said he found it harder and harder to keep up the flow of new ideas.' This pressure was made far worse due to the new commissions that he accepted because of his increased celebrity and popularity with other top acts, in a way harrowingly described by Spike:

'It was a nightmare . . . I had to write a new show every week for six months. If Hitler had done that to someone it would be called torture . . . My crack-up came from overwork, professional problems, and responsibility thrust on to a personality unprepared for it. The madness built up gradually. I found I was disliking more and more people. Then I got to hating them. Even my wife and baby. And then there were the

Michael Bentine was never really replaced.

noises. Ordinary noises were magnified in my brain until they sounded a hundred times as loud as they were, screaming and roaring in my head . . . And the process is so insidious that the awful thing was that I had no idea that I was mentally sick . . . [Finally] I thought, "Nobody is on my side. They are letting me go insane. I must do something desperate so they will put me in hospital and cure me. I know what I'll do. I will kill Peter Sellers." '

Spike's dramatic cry for help worked – his equally melodramatic, loudly announced intention en route to kill Peter (with a potato peeler) generated swift passage to medical care and out of The Goon Show for a large part of that series.

Other people were inevitably called upon to fill the Spike-shaped gap. Jimmy Grafton had always remained an influence of sorts on the later stages of scriptwriting and now found himself called upon much more. Larry Stephens, however, had been a positive influence on scriptwriting technique from the beginning ('Spike used to have the marvellous lively extrovert ideas, and Larry used to bring them down to earth,' Eton recalled). One early BBC picture has all four Goons at a planning session, with Dennis Main Wilson and Jimmy Grafton discussing script with Spike and Larry. Consequently, Larry, who had only recently co-authored a short item with Spike for the Radio Times about the new series, collaborated heavily with Jimmy Grafton to produce the scripts for the next thirteen weeks.

Spike's absence also led to change amongst the performers. Whilst Peter Sellers' mimicry meant that he was able to produce any of Spike's established Goon character voices (as later on in The MacReekie Rising of '74), it was not a good idea to have him talking to himself on a radio show – although a form of experiment along these lines did occur after tape was much more available to the BBC's sound engineers (in 1955). Consequently Dick Emery and Graham Stark, both of whom had a Goon connection from the early days at Graftons of one sort or another, performed on The Goon Show on alternate weeks until Spike was well enough to return. It was the best compromise available to keep the Show on air.

'When Spike was really ill I would bring [Graham or Dick] in,' Eton recalled. 'I had David Jacobs standing by because he was very good with voices . . . I think I only in fact used him once for an Overseas recording. All of these 'standby' people were very good but they couldn't bring the Show right up as the Goons did.''

Peter Eton continued his firm regimen with the Goons, insisting on disciplined rehearsal and rigorous technical run-throughs on the Show. Spike now had more opportunity to develop his 'nonsensical logic' and surreal mind pictures. The

'The world's tallest dwarfs.'

essence of that process? According to Sellers, 'you take an idea, and just let your mind wander: it's the runaway idea. The only way I can describe the form of humour that we enjoy is to say that we take any given situation and carry it to its illogical conclusion.'

'This is the secret ingredient of The Goon Show,' Spike commented once, '– radio, where the pictures are better because they happen on the other side of your eyes.'

Such things were conjured up not only by the dialogue between the Goons but also by various types of sound effect and gramophone record-

Above: Dennis Main Wilson hammering out a contract with the Goons watched by Jimmy Grafton (standing) and Larry Stephens.

Left: The Goons at Cleopatra's Needle on London's Embankment for a press call in 1957.

ing. Eton's drama techniques gave just the tight control that was needed to make them work effectively. 'We loved how you could suggest things by noises; things you can only do on radio. On TV, if a man goes out of frame and you hear a splash you imagine that he has fallen in the water – and you don't need to show it . . . Spike has the ability to use this medium.'

This is what was written as Sound Effects (FX) instruction when one character was offered a cocktail:

Make with the effects of eight jet planes, a police siren, the victim of maniacal strangler, the San Francisco earthquake and the hydrogen bomb. It dies away in a strangled sob and hiss. The verdict on the cocktail follows – 'Quite nice.'

'In the writing side, I always tried to get Spike to do complete melodramas. I preferred this . . . I would give him a basic idea, and then I could influence the script. But if it was just a sketch show where we wandered about all over the place I couldn't exert much influence.' As the third series came to an end The Goon Shows increasingly fell into this Eton-preferred mould.

The discipline was uncompromising. Eton cheerfully referred to the Goons as 'bums' and would stand no nonsense – the fact that he was much in sympathy with what the Show stood for was not allowed to get in the way of professional performance. 'I remember firing Peter Sellers in the middle of a show. We were recording at the Camden Theatre. He did something which put Harry off. In the Max Geldray number I went behind and told him to stick to the script. We went back for the middle spot and he started fooling about again, and I said, 'If you do that again I'll fire you.' He thought I wouldn't dare, so he did it again, so I had to fire him. Later he came back and apologised.'

Mind you, the Goons were not ones to give in without a 'fight'. Eton might rule with a rod of iron in the recording studio but he had to get there first! 'The script was due on the Monday for the show on the following Sunday. It wasn't there one day and I rang up Spike's office, over a greengrocer's shop in Shepherd's Bush . . . [I was told] Spike had left the office with the script. I thought he must be on the booze with Larry so I started looking for him, all round the clubs and pubs where I knew he might be.

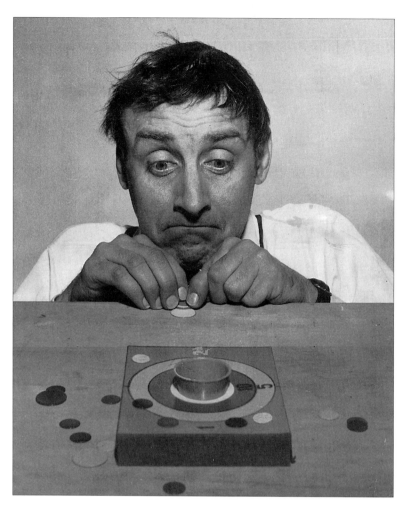

Spike Milligan in tiddlywinks practice . . .

'Later that night I got to the Panama Club. I'd had about twenty beers on the way and I was as tight as a drum. Spike and Larry came in, sober as anything, picked me up and rang Michael Standing [BBC Head of Variety – he knew Eton quite well] and said, 'Peter's drunk, there won't be a show this week.' They were always playing jokes on me . . .'

The Goon Show was gaining in popularity with the listening public. The BBC hierarchy was something else. After all, Milligan's view of Fifties life was sharp focused and uncompromising. On the side of human beings and against the dehumanising influences of society (especially authority) – 'It starts with one man shouting gibberish in the face of authority and proving by fabricated insanity, that nothing could be as mad as what passes for ordinary living.

'The Goons gave me a chance to knock people who my father, and I as a boy, had to call "Sir". Colonels, chaps like Grytpype Thynne with educated voices who were really bloody scoundrels. They'd con and marry rich old ladies; they were cowards charging around with guns.'

Eton strongly supported this. 'The Goons were a strong reaction against the pomposity we all shared during the War. When you see old wartime films on TV you realise how incredibly artificial and pompous we were. People like Spike and Larry tried to cut through this . . . We used to do outrageous things and there were lots of BBC Execs (retired generals, all sorts . . .) who said 'bad taste', especially about anything against the Forces.

'I was nearly sacked because of a joke about OBEs. Peter said to Harry "Have an OBE" or something like that. For that I was hauled up before a board with these old boys sitting round a table and saying we mustn't say this and that . . . It happened altogether about eighteen times and once it was an official reprimand which got entered in my BBC records. John Snagge, who was Head of Announcers and therefore a powerful figure in the BBC in favour of The Goon Show and Milligan's right to creative freedom, would always take me aside afterwards and say, "It's all right Peter, just go away for a while and forget about it."'

Spike would have none of the peacetime self-importance that authority figures took to themselves. It cut no ice at all after being under enemy fire. 'Sir Winston Churchill is the last major politician with a sense of humour. The ones we've got now are ridiculously pompous.' Any and every opportunity to deflate political or bureaucratic ego was taken in the course of putting out a Goon Show.

. . . and in matchplay conditions.

'That tree on Whitehall is going to be cut down. The planners say it's dangerous'
'Why?'
'Well, every time they look, it's still there . . . defying them.'

'We weren't trying to undermine the BBC,' Eton insists. 'We were trying to undermine the "standing order". . . As far as my authority went, yes the Goons tried to undermine that . . . The Director General heard the [naughty Army joke using the name] Hugh Jampton; we put the character in the Radio Times in those days, and I was called up and told off, and instructed not to do it again. Spike knew this so he put it in the next week's script. I cut it out, and they ad-libbed it back in. I meant to cut it out of the tape but it accidentally got left in, and this time I really was in trouble with the hierarchy . . ."

During 1955 and into 1956 Spike struck up a writing partnership with Eric Sykes which ran through most of the Fifth series - some full collaborations, other times strong support from Eric when the pressure of writing threatened to overwhelm Spike. Their friendship remains to this day.

This scriptwriting partnership produced a number of Shows that remained in common memory as Goon classics, such as 'The Dreaded Batter Pudding Hurler' (a solo Milligan effort – the BBC received more than two dozen batter puddings in the post from listeners!), 1985 and 'The Sinking of Westminster Pier'. This latter show also produced once of The Goon Show's most notorious sound effects, Fred The Oyster.

 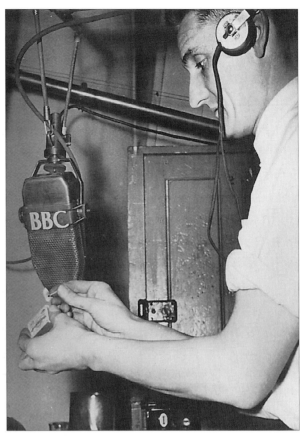

Sound effects played an important part in the humour of the show.

Peter Eton and the Goons took great satisfaction from describing the sound in the most pungent terms possible, thereby achieving the maximum BBC upset. "It was made up for me out of three or four donkey farts played slowly, then speedily and edited . . ." Eton continued to produce The Goon Show until he left the BBC to work in the emerging field of commercial television in 1956. The disciplines he instilled in the Goons for performance were never really lost in the years that remained to the Show, and at their subsequent best such skills were to shine.

Harry and Peter often 'traded' on The Goon Show's popularity in getting bookings during the week in Variety Theatre around the country. This was in fact how their careers advanced while Spike (usually) worked on the next script – the experience was often why they came to look forward so much to the Sunday Goon rehearsals! One series of bookings in Coventry in October 1955 (just after the start of the Sixth Series of The Goon Show), which included Spike, showed what a grim show business roller coaster they were riding.

All three were booked at the Coventry Theatre (ironically, for the Theatre's 'Anniversary Show') with individual acts, as well as a couple of group items. Spike's solo contribution did not go down at all well with this Midlands audience, not even his musical item on the trumpet (at which he was very good). Always to the point he challenged the audience, 'You hate me, don't you?' and received an equally direct response. Spike got more applause for the enraged trampling of his innocent trumpet than the rest of his act.

Stalking off stage, Spike locked himself in his dressing room. Harry and Peter, dressed up ready for a comedy trio act as The Long Itchington Stick Dancers with Spike, sensed big trouble and determinedly gained entry to the changing room. Spike had recently purchased odd items including a grim hangman's noose and it was in the room with him. 'We were dressed with cockney cheesecutter hats with small silver bells, patched roadmenders' trousers with string tied below the knees, more silver bells and large boots,' Harry recalled. 'Every time we charged the door it sounded as if every church tower in the land was having a nightmare.' With Spike kept safe, Peter went on to perform his famous sit-on-stage-and-listen-to-a-record revenge on the audience that had so ruptured Milligan's self confidence.

1956 was a busy year. With the popularity of The Goon Show well established and growing, Spike and Peter in particular looked for different angles on developing Goon humour. Harry was not so prominent in this respect but then during the 1950s his was the busiest and most lucrative individual career of the three. He was much in demand and was also limited by contractual obligation in the kind of things he could do with Spike and Peter. When the Goons released the 'Ying Tong Song' through Decca Records later on in the year, for example, he was only allowed to speak and not sing because he was under contract to Phillips.

The Goons with Ray Ellington, whose musical accompaniment was a regular feature of the show.

Goon humour in sound worked well. What about visually? The Goons had already had one stab at this medium in 1952 in Down Among The Z Men, a project which featured all four original Goons. Unfortunately the filming was undertaken on a tight budget and tighter timetable. A previous 1951 film Penny Points To Paradise, had less success then and fewer viewers since, as film prints were very hard to find. Neither film was able to move much in the surreal fashion of The Goon Show because of the limits of early-1950s film technology. Slapstick comedy was the best compromise they managed.

Still, by 1956 things were slightly better – both Peter and Spike in particular were keen to talk up the prospects. Picturegoer reported:

'. . . conventional screen comedy is in a rut. The humour of conventional screen comedians is forced, their pathos unhealthy . . . For all their talent, they are just following in the footsteps of Chaplin and Harold Lloyd . . . Talking high hat about low comedy, Milligan will say, "There are vast fields of untapped humour. We have used only a fraction of the tricks that the screen can make use of in order to make people laugh. Fantastic, maybe. That's what people said when we started The Goon Show on radio. But we

Spike Milligan and Peter
Sellers in costume.

built up a huge listening audience from practically nothing – without trading on accepted principles.'

Peter made a similar point to Picturegoer when the opportunity presented itself:

' . . . with the right set-up, I think the Goons on film could be startlingly successful, provided that an unconventional technique were used. Certain characters, for example Bluebottle, could not convincingly be humanised – so a form of cartoon on film, seen successfully in an early Gene Kelly musical, might be employed . . . the result might well be a new form of film comedy with an international appeal.'

As it finally appeared in 1956, The Case of the Mukkinese Battlehorn, with Dick Emery as well as Spike and Peter in the main cast, went only part of the way to realising these screen ambitions. Time and budget shortage were again the villains. They would have to wait four more years to strike gold on film.

Nevertheless, 1956 gave still more opportunities. Between February and November (the end of the sixth Series of The Goon Show and the beginning of the Seventh), Peter and Spike became involved in three separate Goon-type television projects for Associated-Rediffusion Television (one of the very few Independent TV projects Spike was ever involved with). Comm-ercial television was still in its infancy and there was no inter-connected network of commercial companies across the UK as there is now. Rather, 'patches' of independent TV existed around the Midlands and London but otherwise viewers could only get BBC programmes – and only one channel of that.

The idea of experimenting with the Goons in vision on the BBC had been mooted by Peter Eton before he left but the hierarchy had not taken the idea up. Consequently overtures were made to A-R TV at the time when it was finding its feet and willing to experiment. This was even more the case since radio was the dominant medium and television the poor relation; TV jumped at the chance of letting established names like Spike Milligan and Peter Sellers attempt to innovate on their franchise.

As a result, viewers were first exposed to The Idiot Weekly Price 2d, a kind of Victorian newspaper edited benignly by Peter, the news items being of a somewhat esoteric nature. Peter was a central and linking figure in the comedy, which involved Spike as well as other supporting actor-Goon-types who had already been involved on the edges of the Goon story, such as Graham Stark. Valentine Dyall, well known from his part as The Man In Black from the radio programme Appointment With Fear, who had become an occasional guest on some radio Goon Show episodes, also became involved. Kenneth Connor, much more often associated with the humour of Carry On films, was closely linked to all three of the television Goon projects and often worked as a counterpart to Graham Stark's roles.

There was a much stronger Goon element in the other two projects. The

next one to bemuse TV viewers was A Show Called Fred, which went to transmission in May. There were ominous warnings from the programme's theme tune of the 'Ying Tong Song' that strange things were about to happen. The Rediffusion gong suffered horribly at the start of each show and the list of cast credits often included some scurrilous inference (such as Kenneth Connor once identified as the rear-end of a pantomime horse).

Sacred cows of the existing TV schedules would be sent up; Max Geldray's musical numbers would be interrupted by genuine Milligan rhythmic tooth tapping or an enthusiastic Sellers 'playing' the soda siphon. Classics of literature would be dismembered – Dr. Jekyll and Mr. Hyde came to an abrupt end when Connor consumed the elixir and was transformed into the resident

A rare picture – three straight-faced Goons. Spike adapted his hairstyle by hand on the photo.

Below: Peter Sellers with his son, Michael.

Bottom: Peter and Spike performing at a charity show in Watford.

female singer. The Count of Monte Cristo's successful rescue of the King collapses into a quick rendition of 'We're Riding Along on the Crest of a Wave'. For viewers in 1956 it must have been innovative viewing – in the style of Monty Python a full thirteen years before that team hit the screen.

Spike continued to push the available technology to its limit in A Show Called Fred and its September sequel, Son of Fred. He used backprojection of images to create a man swimming at powerboat speeds, a boat hurtling down a railway track and a violent volcanic eruption so he could light a cigarette. Other camera tricks were used – Valentine Dyall was seen swinging upside down (or was he?). A small company called Biographic produced cartoon animation solely to interrupt live sketches.

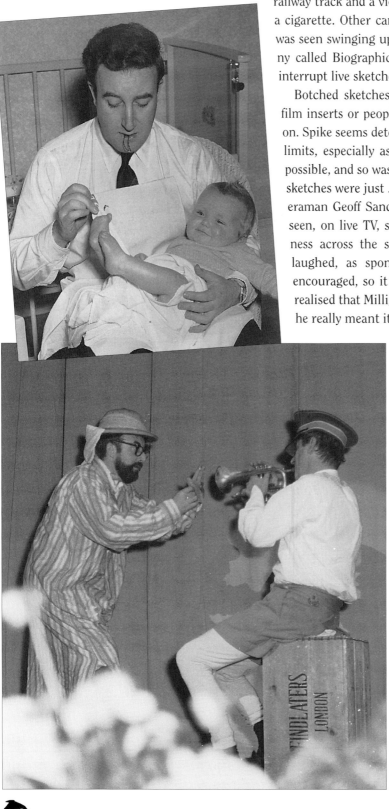

Botched sketches, sketches interrupted by explosions or film inserts or people or crowd inserts . . . the examples go on. Spike seems determined to try and push the format to its limits, especially as Son of Fred was networked as well as possible, and so was being seen by many more people. Some sketches were just . . . well . . . interrupted!. Television cameraman Geoff Sanders recalls a sketch where Milligan was seen, on live TV, swinging upside-down from a stunt harness across the set, shouting 'Get me down!' Everyone laughed, as spontaneous response from the 'set' was encouraged, so it was a couple of minutes before anyone realised that Milligan was shouting 'Get me down' because he really meant it. The harness had slipped out of position and he was actually in real difficulty.

The effort paid off in some ways. Spike received the award for 1956 Best TV Show of the Year for the Fred shows, although he ruefully observed later that "there were only about 350 television sets in England at the time so nobody ever realised." With the ending of the series of Son of Fred however, the Goons' inroads to experimental TV ended. Partly as a result of the fees Spike and Peter could already command, the budgets of the Freds became too stretched to be able to afford further experimental ideas. What's more, the technology still would not stretch far enough, though it had been fun trying.

As though this activity were not enough in 1956, three different Goon singles were released by Decca and Parlophone, some involving collaboration with the bizarrely named Massed Alberts (yes, they had appeared on A Show Called Fred!) –Spike recorded

HARRY SECOMBE · ALFRED MARKS
PETER SELLERS · BILL KERR "PENNY POINTS TO PARADISE"
This copyright advertising material is leased and not sold and is the property of Adelphi Films Ltd. After exhibition this material should be returned to Adelphi Films Limited.
DISTRIBUTED BY ADELPHI FILMS LTD
FREDDIE FRINTON · PADDIE O'NEIL
SPIKE MILLIGAN · JOE LINNANE
D. p. 33.

with them in September, while Peter and Spike recorded two tracks together in May and another two in August – 'I'm Walking Backwards for Christmas' was one of the May tracks, and the famous 'Bloodnok's Rock and Roll Call' one of the other August offerings. Attention then switched back toward the radio Goonery and the Seventh Series. Occasionally a cunning 'plug' for one of the records would be slipped into the Shows by way of an ad lib!

The form of the Goon Show was by now well established. Wallace Greenslade had taken over as BBC continuity announcer from the original Andrew Timothy (who feared for his sanity had he not moved on in mid 1954), and usually suffered some indignity from the Goons. For example:

A publicity shot for the Goons' film, Penny Points to Paradise.

'I have here in my hands, ladies and gentlemen, a chit granting me permission to sing 'Sea Fever' by John Masefield. (piano cue) . . . {sings} 'I must go down to the sea again' – Ooh! (GRAMS: SPLASH)

Scriptwriting was still the product of collaboration between Spike and Larry, although there were more weeks when the entire script was produced by Spike. The characterisations were very well known and very strongly drawn; it was a long time since the performers had been identified in the scripts as themselves,.

Harry was almost entirely Ned Seagoon, or Ned of Wales (it was hard to see where the Secombe ended and the Seagoon began). In this heroic mould he would continue to fall into the villainous influence of Grytpype Thynne or

Pictures used to promote the Peter Sellers vehicle, Let's Go Crazy.

Down Among the Z Men was an early attempt to translate the Goons' humour to the screen.

Above: Sellers and Milligan in the 1956 movie, The Case Of The Muckinese Battlehorn.

Right: Sellers with Dick Emery in a scene from the Muckinese Battlehorn.

Major Bloodnok (both played by Peter) and be inveigled into insuring the English Channel against fire, or some other cunning scheme, until the plot ripened so that he fell victim to it (again).

Around such villainies would orbit the other aspects of Spike's writing that contributed to make The Goon Show such a milestone of radio comedy: the way that logic was turned on its head and made to serve Milligan's already stated purposes – the hilarious but totally pointless arguments between the aged Henry Crun (Peter) and spinster Minnie Bannister (Spike), or the delightful nonsense of Bluebottle and Eccles.

One of the items that shows the strength of Spike's writing is that, although he himself talked about this lack of confidence as a performer in interviews until well after The Goon Show finally ended (Oblomov was a play project of the 1960s after all), all the major Milligan characters (Eccles, Moriarty, Minnie Bannister) sound just as clear, confident and effective in performance as those of Sellers.

Works of literature were far from exempt – parodies of books, films and classic authors gave some strong storylines beyond Peter Eton's time – Beau Geste, She, The Wages of Fear, A Christmas Carol. Many scripts based around Africa held a whiff of parodied Kipling, while the historic British Empire and of course Adolf Hitler's little exploits fuelled many scripts to the end of The Goon Show's days.

As the reputation of The Goon Show and the Goons became more established, special celebrity appearances took place, though the pace of their performing lives did not allow for many, especially as Peter was more in demand. Nevertheless, one celebrity appearance during the Eighth Series run of The Goon Show involved the appointment of the Goons as Royal Champions, on

Peter Sellers in a sketch from *Idiot Weekly*.

behalf of Prince Philip in the Cambridge University Tiddley-winks Championship in March 1958.

The Goons all turned up in suitably scholastic tabards – the whole 'radio team', with Wallace Greenslade, Max Geldray and Ray Ellington as well as Graham Stark, and all wearing ties specially woven for the event. John Snagge, who fought those many high-level battles in the BBC on the Goons'

behalf, was there to inaugurate the challenge himself and read a letter of apology from Prince Philip, who was unable to be with them 'having strained a certain muscle.'

Sadly the Goons were out-tiddled in full view of the Movietone cameras but took their revenge two weeks later in a Goon Show entitled 'Tiddleywinks' in which Seagoon attempts to sabotage the Cambridge team's prospects – he is caught and reprimanded by John Snagge in a prerecorded message. 'Seagoon, you've been a cad. I must ask you, formally, to hand back your tiddleys.'

Another occasion arose around the same time as Harry was featured on This Is Your Life. The rather predictable sequence of set-piece recollections was enlivened by the appearance, at the end, of Peter dressed as Bloodnok, Spike in a sack (as Eccles?), and Ray Ellington – the three of them bringing on a sedan chair for Harry and in which they attempted to carry him off stage. Naturally, it collapsed under him – leading to a hilarious fadeout as Peter and Spike duelled in front of Eamonn Andrews and the bemused Secombe clan . . .

John Browell, who had a longstanding association with The Goon Show – he had had some involvement from the Crazy People days as well as Peter Eton's time – was appointed to take over as producer late in 1958 and kept this position until the final end of The Goon Show. Spike shouldered sole responsibility for the scriptwriting, upon the premature demise of Larry Stephens, for the Ninth Series, and unmistakably demonstrated his mastery of the art. Press

Scenes from A Show Called Fred, written by Spike Milligan in 1956.

reviews and reports of the Goons during late 1958 and 1959 award plaudits and praise that exceeded those already received.

'By 1959,' observed writer Ian Wood, 'The Goon Show had reached its peak, and the team had grown into perfect sympathy with each other, with radio and with their audiences. They had achieved an instinctive knowledge of timing, which every comedian must have . . . knowing how to use an audience . . . how and when to kill a laugh, and how and when to build another on top of it, and few English comedians have ever been able to do this properly. Even Tommy Handley got along mainly on pace, riding over laughs and silences alike . . . By the time the Show ended, the Goons' audience sense had become infallible. They knew exactly when they could horse around, and when the plot had to be carried forward to retain some measure of coherence . . .'

Not only did they know how, but in performance there was a great sense of satisfaction. Witness Peter's comments, reflecting on those times:

'I used to live for those Sundays. Those Sundays, you see, after a week of misery [on the stage] like that. We used to think "how marvellous". That's why, for us, it was such an enormous release. We used to pack such energy into the Show and all our ideas and thoughts went into the Show – everything we had. We were just so keen to let people hear what was going on in our minds – this crazy, strange fantasy . . .'

Alongside that joyous recollection of performance, banished temporarily to the background, was this dark shadow of the effort involved in Spike's act

of creation.

'It cost blood to out that show for me. Sheer agony. It wrecked my first marriage and it wrecked my health. My nervous breakdown happened while I was on the show and I've been a neurotic ever since. So you can say I gave my sanity to that show . . ."

Nevertheless, the energy and lunacy was present right through, from the warm-up. 'Harry was an extremely strong man,' John Browell recalled, 'and he could lift both Spike and Peter up. This was the sort of thing we had during the warm up. Spike would go up with the curtain and hang on to it so that when the curtain went up, his head would go up with it. Mike stands had wheels and they used to use them as scooters. Braces were a favourite, Peter would come along and do the old-time bit – ladies and gentlemen, etc. – and whip away Harry's braces whereupon Peter's trousers would fall down. I tried to get them to do it for the warm-up for the fiftieth anniver-

Peter Sellers deals with his fan mail.

sary Goon Show. Peter cried off, because he remembered the terrible occasion once when they did it and he hadn't got any pants on . . .!"

Some of the shows from 1959 were among the first to be released on a commercial long-playing record, a reflection of the polished, rounded performances that were given at that time. A parody of Quatermass and the Pit was unleashed on an unsuspecting public. Several of these Shows benefited from new sound effects emerging from the recently formed BBC Radiophonic Workshop. It was from here that various slow, musical, pulsating bubbling noises emerged to delight Milligan and Sellers, as well as the impactful radiophonic sound of Major Bloodnok's Stomach undergoing a particularly severe attack of gastric imbalance. When the Goons visited the American West (in a Show entitled 'Call of the West') the Workshop also enabled them to be shot at with new, improved, radiophonic bullets.

Such was the interest of Milligan in the possibilities that this new BBC department offered that there was official reaction (not from John Browell) seeking to prevent the new Workshop from turning into a Goon Show Sound Effects Factory, an attitude which Milligan was powerless to change. As early as 1957 he had begun to complain that limitations of sound were hampering The Goon Show. 'A lot of Goon comedy is pure sound – explosions, bullets whistling, feet clumping. You'd think the BBC could cope with all that. They're supposed to have the greatest record library in the world. But d'you know what

happened the other day? I wanted the sound of wolves howling, and I was told the BBC couldn't help . . .'

Subsequently he let it be known through correspondence in The Listener that fuller access to the Workshop might have extended the life of The Goon Show for a further full series, since by that time he had virtually exhausted every permutation available from the more conventional BBC Sound Library (it subsequently seemed to become a 'factory' for the BBC's Doctor Who instead).

As if there were not enough inspiration around, the Goons could always go 'round the back for the old brandyyyyy!' Harry had introduced the others to this brandy-and-milk concoction, smuggled into the theatre already mixed in a milk bottle. Nobody suspected this brown milk bottle. It did, however, present John Browell with another production hazard. 'I noticed of course from time to time that the bottles of brandy were getting larger and larger, and I used to have to send my staff down there to drink copious quantities of brandy

Spike and Peter block their ears as Kenneth Connor prepares to pop the champagne cork.

Spike reveals the strength of
the German army.

to try and keep the cast sober. I had a sober cast and a drunk staff.'

This run of programmes was not without unexpected incidents. Towards the end of the series, for a script entitled 'The Spy, Or Who Is Pink Oboe', Sellers developed throat trouble and was unable to appear. Whereas, if Spike had been unable to appear Sellers could, at a pinch, produce the necessary voices, it was not at all the same thing in reverse. Four separate performers had to be called in to replace him – Jack Train (from ITMA), Valentine Dyall, Kenneth Connor and Graham Stark.

Worse, for 'The £50 Cure', last one of the series, Harry Secombe became ill with mumps. His telegram to the other Goons read, 'Sorry. Unable to come tonight. Peruvian crut has struck again. Don't drink all the brandy . . .' This last Show of the series had been intended to be the last one forever, with the entire cast and orchestra finally turned into chickens by drinking Henry Crun's transforming laundry bath soup, followed by a heart curdling rendition from all gathered of 'We'll Gather Lilacs In The Spring Again'. Kenneth Connor stood in valiantly for Harry but the intended effect was not quite achieved.

Apart from issues like the Radiophonic Workshop, talk of ending the Show was inevitable. The ambition shared by Harry, Peter, Spike (and Michael) in 1946 had been made popular, viable and a focus for their ambitions and enthusiasms for nearly fourteen years. It had been broadcast for nine years and other pressures were building up. It was getting increasingly difficult to keep the Goons together long enough to record a long series of programmes (there were only seventeen in the Ninth Series instead of the more usual 26).

Peter was more and more in demand in the film industry and had attracted increasing critical interest for his roles in The Ladykillers, The Smallest Show on Earth, tom thumb, The Mouse That Roared and supremely to that point, I'm All Right Jack. All these more notable films were made between 1955 and 1959; in total during those four short years he was involved in nine film projects as a major player (with none at all during 1956, until it was clear that Goonery on TV was not going to develop further). Latterly Peter was being driven from film-set work to Sunday Goon Show rehearsal and back afterwards to keep to schedule! By late 1959 Peter was beginning to absorb this change of emphasis too –

he admitted to CA Lejeune in a magazine interview for the journal Good Housekeeping that 'I think there's more in me than just this Goon Show thing', a comment that the Sellers of 1951 would hardly have believed the 1959 Sellers capable of saying.

What's more, there were problems of direction for the scriptwriting. By the time the Ninth Series was riding high in terms of achievement, over 200 Goon Show programmes had been transmitted. A modest but significant proportion of these Shows were reworkings of ideas used in the very early series and were reworked very effectively (the BBC commissioned Vintage Goons series was also aimed at recovering for overseas use some early scripts). Even so, the strain on Spike of maintaining his own perfectionist standards, increased the more successful he was: 'This was the crucifying part of it. They got better, they became storylines and each story had to be unique.'

The characters upon which the Goon scenarios and comedy largely depended had also developed over the course of the series. Some development had been a gradual decline! As Roger Wilmut has pointed out in detail in The Goon

Peter Sellers as Henry Crun in the Muckinese Battlehorn.

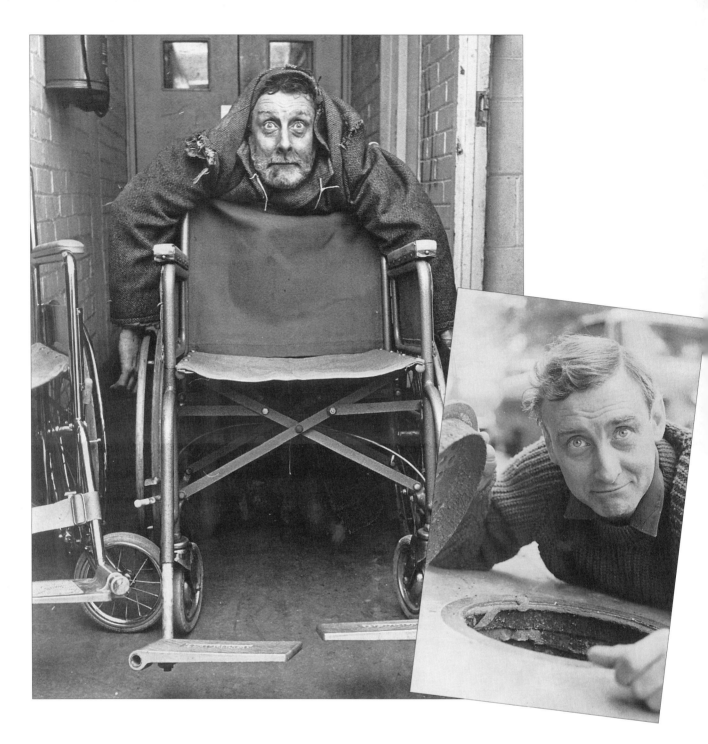

Above: Spike disguised as a wheelchair.

Right: On the trail of a hole.

Show Companion, the most notable examples of this involve Grytpype-Thynne and Moriarty, who are first encountered as highly disciplined and 'respectable' villains in 1953/1954 but by 1959 are impoverished wrecks, foraging for accommodation, money and food (though not necessarily in that order) usually at the expense of Seagoon, who still didn't see the inevitable payoff coming. They were a sign of the times that Spike recognised. 'The Show was starting to degenerate . . . It had to come to an end . . . There was one more throw of the dice to go and I think if we had thrown it we would have gone down and been forgotten. We got out while we were right on top.'

In point of fact, the response of the listening public was so strong to the prospect of the programme ending that the BBC were almost compelled to negotiate a further series, which enabled The Goon Show to creep into the 1960s. Again, although Spike had seen warning signs, the Goons still performed Shows to a standard that could be issued almost immediately on LP record, in this case Tales of Men's Shirts. Even so, by halfway through the com-

missioned series The Goon Show ended with, appropriately, 'The Last of the Smoking Seagoons' on 28 January 1960. Spike did not attempt to round off the characters' histories as he had done at the end of the Ninth Series. There was just Greenslade saying, 'Yes, that was it – the last of them, so 'bye now!'

THE LAST
GOON SHOW OF ALL

ANDREW   Ladies and gentlemen, we have had a large num-
          ber of telegrams wishing us, believe it or not, good
          luck...and heaven only knows we need it. There is
          only time to recall one of them, and may I read it
          to you. It is addressed, of course, to the Goons and
          the message is as follows . . . 'One of your most
          devoted fans is enraged at the knowledge that he
          is missing your last performance. Last night my
          hair fell out and my knees dropped off having
          turned green with envy at the thought of my
          father and sister attending the show. One day,
          perhaps, you will find time to give a performance
          for a shipful of Seagoons. My very best wishes, as
          always, signed . . . Charles'

ORCHESTRA   (Variety of tuning up sounds. Conductor taps
             baton on music stand. Orchestra responds by pro-
             ducing batons and tapping on music stands.)

SPIKE   (whispers to others) One, two, three...

ALL   Variety of welcome, thank you speeches, all unin-
          telligible.

ANDREW   They haven't quite got the hang of it yet, but after

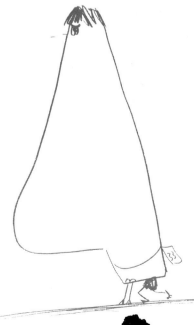

another smoke they should get be switched on. If you are switched on, I am empowered by the governors of the BBC wireless to say 'Good Evening' in that order. I also have it on good authority that my name is Clapham Junction, but I'll have that checked out later. When I announced the first Goon Show in a field off Tiverton, I was 30 . . . I am now 93. Mr Sellers will now sell a gross of his cars and take up a dramatic voice.

PETER   Oh, yes, yes, yes. I have been asked by the Beeb Beeb Ceeb to get the audience warmed up. Well, to the best of my knowledge, there is no better way than by the gentlemen using their right hand to squeeze the top of the lady's thigh next to them...

ALL   Oh, aah, oooh, ah, ooooh!

PETER   Splendid! I will now whistle the soliloquy from Hamlet (whistles 'To be or not to be')

ANDREW   That was Mr Sellers practising his comeback. This morning BBC archives delivered three coffins. I will now introduce the contents of coffin number one...bald, toothless and weighing 37 stones - Harry Secombe!

ORCHESTRA   (Rousing showbiz intro theme.)

HARRY   (through megaphone) Thank you! Hello, folks of the world. I am speaking to you using the new aluminium cone voice projector. I will start my comeback with a new trick taught to me by a one-legged sailor who did toffee apple impressions for Noel Coward (puts finger in mouth and makes popping noise). Did you hear that? (repeats popping noise). That's it folks! It's the new Grateful Dead Seagoon sound. I will now reveal the secret to the world live via satellite from Neasden. Take the index finger, stick it in the gob, slide gently forward inside the cheek giving it an added impetus as it shoots forward from the lips – so! (repeats popping). See? We directors of Harlech Television are not as daft as you think!

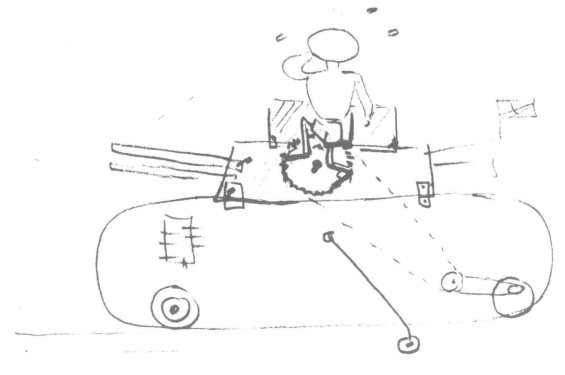

ANDREW   During that demonstration of Mr Secombe's senility – a smile, a song and a wheelchair – the remains of Mr Spike Milligan, the well-known typing error, have been reassembled and he makes this sound...

GRAMS   (Nazi chant) Sieg Heil! Sieg Heil! Sieg Heil!

SPIKE   Policemen are numbered in case they get lost!

PETER   (Stan Laurel voice) I say, Ollie, anyone with a name like Hitler can't be all that bad.

SPIKE   (Heavy German accent) Zere iss anozzer fine mess you haff got us in to.

GRAMS   (Nazi chant speeds off into oblivion.)

ANDREW   As everybody knows who reads the Isle of Arran Shoemakers' monthly, Her Majesty the Queen was to have opened this Goon Show but owing to a nasty rumour called Grocer Heath, she has declined. However, at short notice and wearing floral creton frock, Mr Secombe has agreed to stand in for the Sovereign.

Croonaphant

HARRY	Ladies and gentlemen, my first impression for the Queen will be a hedgehog doing acupuncture on Yul Brynner's nut.Oh-ah-ooh-ah-ooh-ooh-!(fades off).
HENRY+MIN	Get on . . . please . . . hurry . . . get on with it
HARRY	What–what–what–what–what?
HENRY	Start the show...hurry.
HARRY	Hurry? Why?
HENRY	We're dying...
FX	Nuts, bolts, hitting the floor.
HARRY	What was that?
HENRY	Mnk...Min falling to bits...She's a loose woman you know...
HARRY	Throw a bucket of water over her before the season starts . . . And now, ladies and gentlemen, my husband and I have great pleasure in starting Goon Show number 161!
GRAMS	(Sound of sluggish engine turning over unsuccessfully.)
HARRY	Oh. My husband and I have great pleasure in starting this Goon Show number 161!

A Twit

144

GRAMS   (Sound of dodgy engine failing again to start.)

HARRY   My husband and I are having great difficulty in starting Goon Show number 161.

PETER   (strange Michael Caine voice) 'Ello, 'ello,'ello,'ello,'ello.

HARRY   Ah! A constable of Old England played by an ageing Peter Sellers.

PETER   I'm sorry sir, you cannot park that huge bloated Welsh body there.

HARRY   Watch it, Rozzer.

PETER   I 'ave been watchin', sir, and it gives me no pleasure . . . there's not many people know that. What is your name sir?

HARRY   Harry Secombe.

PETER   What a splendid memory you've got. Now then sir, would you like to explain as to why you are wearin' a flowered criton frock?

HARRY   Explain?

PETER   Yes.

HARRY   Haven't you read the court circular?

PETER   No, I'm waitin' till they make the film of the book of the street of the play.

HARRY   Now listen, constable.

PETER   Yes.

HARRY   I am dressed like this because I have been asked to represent Her Majesty the Queen.

PETER   Oh, I'm sorry, Your Queen. My refund ferpologies

HARRY   It's too late for that.

PETER   It's only 'alf past five.

HARRY   We're having difficulty starting this Goon Show.

PETER   Well, let's have a look in the tonk, then. Tonk? Ah, I see you've still got the same typist you 'ad in 1953 . . .

HARRY   Yes, I still have her, no one's found out yet.

PETER   Yes, 'ere's the trouble, Your Queen. There's no jokes in the fuel tonk.

HARRY   I'll just shout a few in. I say! I say! I say!

SPIKE   What d'you say? What d'you say?

HARRY   How do you start a pudding race?

SPIKE	I don't know, how do you start a pudding race?
HARRY	sago.
GRAMS	(Donkey braying and farting.)
SPIKE	Someone get me out of here!
HARRY	I say! I say! Can a lady with a wooden leg change a pound note?
SPIKE	Can a lady with a wooden leg change a ten pound note? Yes!
HARRY	No, she can't.
SPIKE	And why not?
HARRY	Altogether folks – she's only got half a knicker!
ORCHESTRA	(Bad chord).
ANDREW	The plague hit London in 1546 and has been here ever since – Mrs Dale's last husband, Ray Ellington!

RAY SINGS TENNESSEE WALTZ

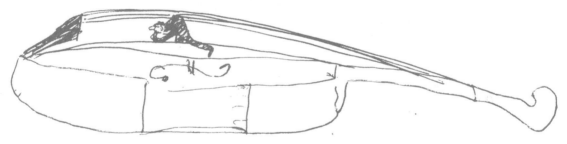

ANDREW	That was Ray Ellington, one-time colour sergeant, now a Chelsea pensioner.
GRAMS	Clockwork engine noise.
NED	(sings)If I ruled the world, every day would be . . .
MORIARTY	Sapristi Ruckus! Here comes Neddie driving an unlicensed Goon Show with CD plates on.
G-T	Smails of loon! It does look a bit seedy, doesn't it? Yes, he's dressed as our Gracious Queen. There must be trouble at the Palace!
NED	Ahoy there gentlemen of the frog and throad. Have you seen a knighthood go this way?
G-T	Yes, but Richard Attenborough was wearing it, and anyway it was the wrong size for that huge, bloated Welsh body of yours.
NED	What-what-what-what-what? Mind what you say or we will have you incarcerated!
G-T	The unkindest cut of all. Ned, just relax against this cut–throat razor. Neddie, now just listen to this...

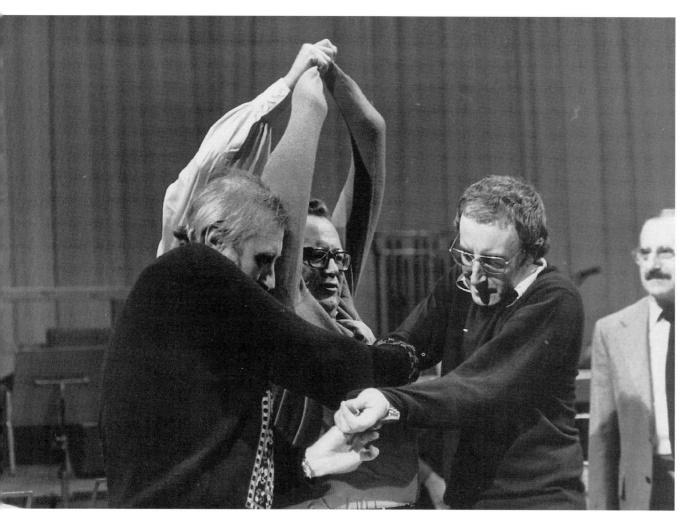

GRAMS   (high speed, squeaky voice) This is what you do...

G-T   You see that's what's happened to Milligan. You don't want to end up like that. Here is a preview of next winter in Jimmy Grafton's attic...

GRAMS   (howling stormy wind)

G-T   There! Can your legs stand another recorded winter like that?

NED   Well, I don't stand all winter. Sometimes I lie down...depends on who she is...

G-T   Ned, making love with cold legs up can cause knee trembling and ruin a man's chances in the old wedding stakes there.

NED   Oh. What do you suggest?

G-T   Leg-lag!

NED   Leg-lag?

G-T   Leg-lag!

MORIARTY   Leg–argglah!

G-T   Let me introduce that. A Frenchman of noble birth, the family arms a rack rampant on a field of steaming argent tat, voted actor of the year by Mrs Mable Fumes, son of the eminent crapologist and swine, Count Dingleberries Moriarty!

MORIARTY   I tell you there is a curse on the house of Moriarty!

NED   What is it?

MORIARTY   The Hampstead Building Society!

NED   He looks in a bad way. Has he had a medical check?

G-T   Yes, thirty shillings for a new truss.

NED   I command you, lag my legs!

MORIARTY   mon . . maddock . . mnk . . .

ORCHESTRA   (Royal leg–lagging fanfare.)

G-T   That will be one hundred pounds in war gratuities and thirty new pence for the fanfare.

FX   (Cash Register)

G-T   Thank you, Neddie. I will now adjust my address before doing a moonlight. Moriarty, get out the Land Rover and measure his legs.

MORIARTY   Now, lift up your trousers, Neddie.

FX   (Sound of roller blind rolling up.)

BLUEBOTTLE   Ooooh-he-heee! Who pulled those trousers up?

MORIARTY   Name of a dog! Rover! Le garçon Bottle is there avec spots.

BLUEBOTTLE   Oooh, it's Moriarty! You've gone bald. What is that lump on your nut?

MORIARTY   That is the difference between margarine.

BLUEBOTTLE   I know what we can do. Let's play mothers and milkmen and Neddie can be the bluetit that pecks the top of the cream. Peck! Peck! Peckee! Oooh- he-hee! Oh, I've hurted my groin again...

NED   Bluebottle you little devil! What were you doing up my trousers?

BLUEBOTTLE   A man has to do what a man has to do...an' I did it over there.

NED   Come out of my trousers at once, you spotty Herbert.

BLUEBOTTLE   My name is not Herbert. I am James Bottle, double 0 seven and three–quarters cop size – ace reporter for the hard-hitting, brown-paper Junior Hours.

NED   Get out, or I'll fetch you one.

BLUEBOTTLE   I can fetch it myself. Don't shout at me please. I have got two 'O' levels and a budgerigar.

NED   I say. What are you doing with that budgerigar?

BLUEBOTTLE   I have got certain unsavoury snaps of your bloomers.

NED   What-what-what-what-what? But I–I have to wear them, you see. that's protocol.

Little Jim

BLUEBOTTLE	Oooh, what have you been eating?
NED	Give me back those snaps, or I'll never be on Stars on Sunday again, you know.
FX	(Door slams followed by frantic knocking.)
NED	Bluebottle! Open this trouser door or I'll break every bone in my fist!
BLUEBOTTLE	I'm not coming out until you give me a postal order for twenty new pence made out to Molly Quots.
NED	Oh, folks! How could I raise that amount? I know. I could go and play variety in merry Blackpool. I can still remember that shaving routine. How does it go again . . .?
ANDREW	Mr Secombe's departure from the mike is a timely one – any departure of his is timely. I have a grave announcement to make. Just before this show started, Mr Max Geldray died. His wife described his condition as satisfactory. However, by waving some money under his nose, he has recovered enough to play his probate.
	Max Geldray accompanied by his orchestra
GRAMS	(Clucking of chickens and tuning of piano continues in background).
HENRY	(vaguely in tune with piano tuning) Mmnk... Ummm... Hnaaa...
MIN	Henreee!
HENRY	What, Min, what?
MIN	Where are you, Henry?
HENRY	I'm inside the new easy rider piano, Min.
MIN	Speak up, Henry! Eric Sykes is in. Which piano are you in, Henry?
HENRY	I'm in the mahogany, lattice-fronted, iron-framed upright, serial number 935427D.
MIN	Oooh...They don't write numbers like that any more.
FX	(Cluck, quack, meow. Cluck, quack, meow.)
HENRY	Min. Listen Min. That was a chicken-duck-cat.
MIN	Oh dear. Does it lay eggs?
HENRY	No, it lays kittens.
ORCHESTRA	(Breathless variety theme.)
GRAMS	(Thunderous explosions, machine gunning, cavalry trumpet.)
BLOODNOK	Oh! Oh! What's going on? Get her out the back. Where's me spares? The laundry will never keep up with this, you know.

Bloodnok II

GRAMS	(Sound of incoming artillery shell followed by more explosions).
NED	Bloodnok, stop that!
BLOODNOK	Yes, which way did it go? It-it's a lady! Can it be? Yes! (sings) It's my dear little Alice Bluegoon...
RAY	Bloodnok! Come out and fight! Surrender the fort!
BLOODNOK	I can't! It's leasehold and Lichfield and Grosvenor Estates and all that. Cheques and postal orders only . . .
NED	Who's that out there laying the part of Ray Ellington?
BLOODNOK	It's my mortal enemy, the Red Bladder. Go away, Bladder, and find your own television series!
RAY	Bloodnok, you coward!
BLOODNOK	You can't call me a coward and get away with it!
RAY	You big coward!
BLOODNOK	He got away with it!
GRAMS	(Explosion)
BLOODNOK	Duck, Neddie!
FX	(Quack. Phone rings. Receiver is lifted.)
BLOODNOK	Hello? What? Yes!

FX   (Receiver slammed down).

BLOODNOK   That was the Beeb Beeb Ceeb. They've switched Goon Shows. This is now number 162.

GRAMS   (Gunfire).

MILLIGAN   (Indian accent) Pardon me, sir.

BLOODNOK   What is it, Private Parts? It is Private Parts, isn't it?

MILLIGAN   No sir. I am Singiz Thing.

BLOODNOK   Singiz Thing? I remember you very well, yes. What do you want?

MILLIGAN   It's time for your perversion, sir.

BLOODNOK   My perversion? Good! Good, let's start now...

GRAMS   (Wailing, groaning, whipping, straining, operatics, crashing, tinkling, thumping, ecstasy). [Continues over Bloodnok]

BLOODNOK   Ah! Oh! I love a bit of Wagner. Now the whips! Yes! Yes! Oh! Ah! Let me have the strot flicker now, I like that. Oh! Yes! Ah! Now the steering wheel club followed by the...oh! Is it all over? What about the starters? Now then, this uniform goes back to Moss Bros tomorrow.

MILLIGAN   Yes, sir. There is a deposit on it.

BLOODNOK   Oh, that'll brush off, don't worry about that. Now, Ned, why are you wearing that lovely creton frock? You're not the relief column, are you?

NED   Take your hands off me and place them higher up.

BLOODNOK   Oh, that's where it's all happening is it?

NED   I'm dressed like this for Goon Show number 161.

GRAMS   (Cheers)

BLOODNOK   Listen to that. My pension's got through. Look, Ned, you need a rest. There's only one place. Go down into the coal cellar and do it down there.

FX   (Dripping in noise in damp cellar. Also, strange munching noise.)

NED   I wasn't sure, but I swore I could hear what sounded like someone eating coke.

ECCLES   (sings) Dum–dum, da–da–rum. Dere are tree men in my life. To one I am a mudder, to de udder I'm a wife. De third one gets the best...

NED   Who's that? Who's that? Who's that?

ECCLES   Dat's you.

NED   I know it's me! The creature was wearing a mini coal sack, both feet in one army boot and a coal scuttle on his head. He must be one of ours!

ECCLES   Glad I'm not one of dem.

NED   What are you doing down here?

ECCLES   Everybody's got to be somewhere.

NED   Yes, but who are you?

ECCLES   Oooh, da hard ones first, eh? Now, I don't want you to spread this around . . . I'm the coal man.

NED   Coal man? It's three in the morning.

ECCLES   Yup. It's never too late to be a coal man.

NED	What I mean is, after you deliver coal, you're supposed to go back to the cart.
ECCLES	Oooh. You mean I should have let go of the sack?
NED	Yes.
ECCLES	But they said they were giving me the sack. I wondered why the job didn't last long. Must be the old Finchley Exchange tomorrow morning.
NED	How long have you been down here?
ECCLES	Oooh. I kept a record. I scratched every day on de wall.
NED	Good heavens! The walls are covered in them, and so are you...suits you.
ECCLES	Thank you, sailor.
NED	You've only scratched six days to a week.
ECCLES	Yup. Don't believe in working on Sundays.
NED	Where's that drip coming from?
ECCLES	Dat's me. I'm leaking. Here, are you a plumber man?
NED	No, I'm standing in for Buckingham Palace. Help me and I'll make you a companion of Honor Blackman.
ECCLES	Wow–ho–ho–ho–hoooo!
NED	Stop that or you'll go blind, I tell you! Listen, I'm going to have a royal kip. Now, if you see anybody come out of my trouser door – belt him. Now good-night England and the Colonies. I'll just put on this record of royal snoring.

FX	(Snores.)
ECCLES	Dat's what money can do for you, folks.
BLUEBOTTLE	Pssssst...
ECCLES	What?
BLUEBOTTLE	Psssst?
ECCLES	I haven't touched a drop.
BLUEBOTTLE	Eccles, it's me Blinbuttons.
ECCLES	Oh, my friend!
BLUEBOTTLE	You remember me?
ECCLES	I remember you.
BLUEBOTTLE	Yes...Why do you not open the door?
ECCLES	Okay, I'll open...how do you open a door?
BLUEBOTTLE	You turn the knob on your side.
ECCLES	I haven't got a knob on my side.
BLUEBOTTLE	On the door!

ECCLES	Oh, the door. I'll soon get the hang of dat.
FX	(Door opens).
BLUEBOTTLE	Well, Eccles . . .
LITTLE JIM	Pah...pilton pa de dee pin pah...etc.
BLUEBOTTLE	I say, Eccles.
ECCLES	What?
BLUEBOTTLE	What is that sticking out of the top of your boot wearing a cap?
ECCLES	This is my nephew, Little Jim.
BLUEBOTTLE	Oh, hello, Little Jim.
LITTLE JIM	Pah...pilta pa de dee pin pah...etc.
ECCLES	He says he doesn't understand what he's saying either.
BLUEBOTTLE	He's one of Mrs Thatcher's Incomprehensives.
NED	(Snores.)
BLUEBOTTLE	Here, who is that snoring in the frock?

ECCLES	Dat's de new sound. It's Neddie. He thinks he's the Queen of England.
BLUEBOTTLE	Yee–hee–hee! Eccles, let's play a game and push him down a well...
ECCLES	Yeah,,,
BOTH	Hup!
NED	Aaaaaaaaaarggh!!!
GRAMS	(Huge splash.)
LITTLE JIM	Oooh...he's fallen in the water!
GRAMS	(Explosions).
BLOODNOK	Oh! Oh! Out of me way! The Red Bladder's after me.
NED	Hold it!
BLOODNOK	I can't hold it much longer. It's old age.
G-T	Your Majesty, good news. We have just found Goon Show number 163 in which you play the lead all the way through as an underfloor heating detective.
MORIARTY	Now, Neddie, just get under these nice floorboards.
FX	(Floorboards hammered down).
NED	Help! And I mean that sincerely.
BLUEBOTTLE	Here, where are you? Do not frighten me, I have got clean underwear on.
NED	Help! I'm in a play under the floorboards.
BLUEBOTTLE	Oh. You must have got a real bad agent.
NED	Get me out!
BLUEBOTTLE	Yes...I can see your belly through the knothole. Oooh...poke, poke, pokey!
NED	Stop that poking!
BLUEBOTTLE	That was a different show, you twit. This show is number 164. This is where I say roll up, roll up! Sixpence for a quick stick to poke Neddie Seagoon. Poke–poke–pokey!
NED	Stop that poking, I tell you!
BLUEBOTTLE	Pokey-pokey!
BLOODROK	Out of my way!
GRAMS	(Big Ben chimes, bagpipes, church bells).
BLOODROK	What's going on, I demand to know...
ORCHESTRA	(Theme tune).
ANDREW	That was The Goon Show, a specially recorded programme for the 50th anniversary of the BBC, starring Peter Sellers, Spike Milligan and Harry Secombe. You also heard the Ray Ellington Quartet, Max Geldray and the orchestra conducted by Peter Knight. Script by Spike Milligan. Produced by John Browell.

ERIC SYKES' STORY

When Eric Sykes first encountered the Goons, he was languishing in a hospital bed recovering from a major ear operation. The effects of the anaesthetic and the vigilance of a hospital matron, whom you can't help thinking must have looked a bit like Hattie Jacques, are all that saved the helpless Sykes from the manic bedside manner of Spike Milligan and Larry Stephens.

'What happened was that I'd heard a show broadcast on the radio. It wasn't The Goon Show then, it was The Crazy People. I listened in to it while I was in hospital and I thought it was the most refreshingly funny stuff ever to come out on radio. I was really incredibly keen, so I did something which I would never normally have done and wrote to Spike Milligan to tell him how much I had enjoyed the programme.

'It was quite a long letter about my impressions of the show and a few suggestions because Spike was a new writer and I was pleased to have a new writer like Spike join the ranks of the comedy writers because there weren't so many of us at that time and I wanted to give him some encouragement.

'I didn't expect an answer to the letter, but the day I had my operation, I was just coming out of the anaesthetic when the door opened and these two very white faces appeared. They looked so white because I had bandages all round my head. The matron came and shooed them away, so I never got to talk to them then, which is just as well because I was still heavily sedated.'

Spike and Larry were nothing if not persistent, however, and, determined to meet the country's foremost comedy writer, they turned up at the hospital

Eric Sykes, an inspiration to the Goons.

Eric collaborated with Spike on some of the scripts.

again the next day.

'They came back once I had recuperated a bit and Spike said, 'Coming from you, that letter was such an inspiration to us' and he thanked me, which was rather nice'

Having listened to The Crazy People, Eric had no doubts about its potential. He also realised how anxious Spike was to impress.

'When Spike and Larry Stephens wrote those first Goon Shows I knew they had a success. I remember thinking 'Thank God we have another writer,' because the more good writers, the better the standard of comedy is going to be.

'Spike was a very funny man but I thought he was a bit hyperactive and trying desperately hard to make sure that everything he said was funny instead of just relaxing. I remember thinking that he would learn, when he became more accepted as a writer, to enjoy his leisure hours instead of going round with a placard on him saying 'I am a funny man'

Eric knew Harry Secombe quite well as Harry had worked on Educating Archie and Peter Sellers was also a reasonably familiar figure, so he was fascinated to see how these three distinctly different individuals worked together.

'Spike was the only unknown quantity at first, but by the time I was writing with him I knew them all very well. Harry was very funny, bouncy and buoyant. He literally bounced into a room and lit it up with joy and happiness. He had a wonderful voice, too. You could hear him half a mile away even if he was only saying 'No thank you.' He was the core around which The Goon Show was set.

Eric and Harry about to depart on a trip to Uganda together.

'Spike had his brilliance with writing and Peter had his brilliance with characters. Each of them were totally different to one another but they dovetailed so beautifully. Those three people were enough. When you put an orchestra behind them, you had the show.'

It is widely acknowledged that The Goon Show was a new departure in comedy and the seemingly free-form style of humour practised by the Goons led many to believe that they were virtually making up lines as they went along. But, as a writer and performer, Eric understood the painstaking effort which went into constructing the show and warns against trying to imitate such a style without having first done the spadework.

'A lot of young comics now like to say, 'Oh, I just go on stage and improvise.' That is impossible. You can't have a theatre full of people who have paid good money to see somebody and then you go on and hope to improvise. When you improvise, you can't guarantee success. You can't guarantee it's going to be funny – you have to have written something.

'The Goon Show sounded like it was all just cobbled together and they were saying the first thing that came into their heads, but that's the secret of good writing. The script was all written down and they were actually standing there reading it.

'When Spike finished his script, or I handed in a script when I was involved, it was nearly all there – every word. There was nothing haphazard about it and there was very little room for any unscripted improvisation or ad-libs. You cannot improvise in a show that is only 25 or 30 minutes long. The show has to finish on time and it is difficult enough assessing how much time the laughter is going to take up. You could start to improvise and have the audience roaring

Top: Despite what is sometimes thought, the Goons rarely departed from the script.

Above: Eric with his wife, Edith.

with laughter and then find that you've run out of time but you'd still got ten minutes of script left to do. There was a lot of discipline involved in The Goon Show and the strength of the show was that it sounded like indiscipline.

'People say of me now, when I'm on stage and crack a gag, 'Oh, yeah, I bet that wasn't in the script', but you can bet your sweet life I say it every night. That was the beauty of working with Jimmy Edwards in a show called Big Bad Mouse. A lot of it sounded like ad-lib, but we had been doing that stuff for years. The art of it is to make it sound as if it is the first time anybody's heard it.

'For any comic to say that they just improvise, that they go on stage and go on the attack, is all rubbish. I think that putting that idea in the minds of young comics, and young people who want to be comics, is a very dangerous thing. Comedy is one of the lowest forms of art, but it's one of the most difficult to master.'

Without doubt, the Goons mastered their art. Eric believes that the journeyman with whom they served their apprenticeships deserves some of the

credit for the success of his protégés.

'Jimmy Grafton was one of the driving forces behind the Goons. They used to meet up in his pub in Whitehall, but he not only provided a meeting place, he had also been a Major in an infantry regiment and he had a distinguished war record. Well, Spike and Harry still talk about the war as if it was yesterday. Jimmy never talked about it much, but there was a lot of hero worship towards Jimmy from Spike and Harry. They used to go to the pub and have a lot of laughs and I think that it was Jimmy who thought that they should harness this. In all fairness, I think that, if not the driving force, Jimmy was certainly the collection point for the Goons.

'I have never really been a fan of the word 'Goon'. That came from the prisoner of war camps in Germany where the prisoners referred to the German guards as goons. I like it better than zany people or mad or crazy, but it's always felt a bit awkward.'

Having worked with and written for some of the top performers of the day, including Frankie Howerd, Eric is far more aware of the range of comedy acts which were around in the fifties but still finds it difficult to compare the Goons with any of their contemporaries.

'Stage comedy came in the form of farces or vaudeville, which is another facet of the business. It came from comics who had an act they had honed over 40 years. They usually only had two acts and both of them were so beautifully honed down that if you wanted to learn about comedy, you went to see them.

'The advent of radio brought comedy into people's lives in a totally different way. It was an entirely new medium and you cannot take a stage act and transfer it straight onto radio, just as today you cannot take a stage act and put it on television. They are all different media.

Top: Some of the leading performers of the day: Bernard Bresslaw, Bruce Forsyth, Arthur Haynes, Harry Secombe and Eric Sykes.

Above: Spike Milligan in 1962.

John P Hamilton creating Goons sound effects in 1954 with his script on a music stand.

'When The Goon Show came along, I would rate the major shows on radio as being Take It From Here and Educating Archie but I would rate The Goon Show above both of them because it was breaking completely new ground as far as characters were concerned – and they were doing it specifically for radio.

'Between them, Spike and Peter Sellers created characters which represented every aspect of life in Britain as we knew it, from the idiot to the do-gooder and the incredibly aged like Minnie and Crun to crooks like Grytpype Thynne. Eccles was honest but thick and Bluebottle was keen but hopeless. Unlike other shows, you didn't always have the same five characters every week and, despite their familiar traits, these characters were from another world.

'The Goon Show was the number one fun show on radio. How does it compare with contemporary shows on radio, stage or television? This cannot be done.'

While it may not be possible to make any sensible comparison between the Goons and other acts, the sources from where Spike drew inspiration are easier to define.

'Spike used to enjoy reading books by a Canadian author called Stephen Leacock. The way the books were written, they were almost like Goon Shows and I think he had a great influence on Spike. In Educating Archie, I think I was one of the first people to try to create mental pictures on radio using lots of sound effects. Spike took this idea of sound effects and raised it to another level altogether. He would use the sound of a jet engine for someone going from A to B. That sort of thing was a new innovation, something that nobody else was doing.'

Eric not only influenced and encouraged Spike's writing, they shared an office. This led to a collaboration which produced some classic Goon Show scripts, and some dangerous moments.

'When Spike and I shared an office in Shepherd's Bush, I was writing a lot for Frankie Howerd as well as doing Educating Archie while he was working on The Goon

Show. He was quite exhausted and asked me if I would help him out with the shows.

'In some respects it was fun but in others it was fraught with danger. On one occasion we argued all day about one word. He said that without the word the line would not work and I said it would work anyway. He said it wouldn't and I said it would until eventually he threw a paperweight at me which missed me and went through the window – and we were on the fifth floor.

'I went down through the apples and cabbages of the greengrocer's shop above which we worked, retrieved the smashed paperweight – it was a kind of pot – and brought it back upstairs. I put it down on the desk and said, 'Don't ever forget what day this was.' Of course, Spike started to blotch up. That was the first disagreement we ever had – all over one word.

'We wrote together for a few shows and then eventually I wrote one week and he wrote the next week, giving us a fortnight to finish a script.'

Eric has always been reluctant to take much credit for writing The Goon Shows, although he was involved for two seasons and whole or partly responsible for at least two dozen scripts. He claims that the foundations laid by Milligan made writing Goon Shows a delight – all he had to do was copy Spike's style.

'If you are a good writer with a bit of confidence, you should have enough of an instinct to be able to copy somebody else's style. Rembrandt and Michelangelo didn't paint every bit of their pictures. They had students who would finish off bits and pieces like the cherub's feet or something. Some of those students could probably do a very passable impression of Rembrandt or Michelangelo. That's what I was doing. As far as I was concerned, writing Goon Shows was an absolute gift. All the characters were there and all I had to do was give them their ration of air time.'

Apportioning the appropriate number of lines to each character could have been a problem if Eric had lacked the discipline to avoid dwelling

Eric and Spike in Johnny Speight's TV series Curry and Chips in 1969.

165

Eric with Hattie Jacques in a
scene from Sykes Big Big Show.

on his favourite.

'Major Bloodnok was my favourite because he was so obviously a failure but
so full of bombast. He'd sell his own grandmother down the river if the price
was right and I think that with all his failings he was destined to end up in some
doss-house or in cardboard city.

'I remember when Spike and I were writing the show together we spent a
whole morning laughing at a little bit we had written for Bloodnok. We laughed
until there were tears streaming down our faces. Sometimes when you write
you hit a vein of gold and that was a real motherload. We laughed all morning

and many bottles of wine were then consumed at Bertorelli's, just across the road next to the funeral parlour.'

Having written many long-running shows for stage, TV and radio, Eric understands the pressure involved in meeting tight deadlines and maintaining a high standard of writing, but he didn't really appreciate the effect that the stress of writing The Goon Show was having on Spike.

'I know that by the time he asked me if I'd help him out, Spike was just about ready for the knackers' yard. He was reaching the end of his tether and that's the only reason I agreed to do it. I really had enough of my own work to do. I was writing full time and discussing new ideas with Galton and Simpson and Johnny Speight, so we didn't really have time to look round and smell the roses.'

Eric was not impressed with the way the BBC handled Spike, although he does have a healthy respect for some of the backroom boys and the support they gave to The Goon Show.

'Most things that Spike has done have not been well understood by the BBC hierarchy. The Goons wasn't an ordinary, gentle, Barbara Cartland sitcom. It was more like anarchy and because they didn't understand it, I'm sure they thought that the sooner the public tired of it the better. Then they could get back to 'Hello, is your father up yet?' and enter in from the French windows.

'Seemingly uncontrolled anarchy' – the Goons.

'The effects department at the BBC were tremendous, though. Neither The Goon Show nor Educating Archie would have been half as successful without a good effects department.

'As far as the producers on the show are concerned, I think that Peter Eton was excellent. Dennis Main Wilson was also excellent. I don't think there was anything to choose between the two. Dennis Main Wilson's great strength on all the different shows I did with him over the years was his tremendous enthusiasm. That drove everybody on and whichever show he was producing was the best show he'd ever worked on and the artists were the most brilliant in the world. That means a lot because all of us artists and writers are inwardly very poor creatures and any little pat on the head is greatly welcomed.'

'Sometimes, however, when things weren't working out too well, his boundless enthusiasm could be a bit too much. I would say 'Dennis, for goodness sake go and make the tea' because he was making me smile and I knew that I hadn't got anything to smile about!'

Eric was not the only writer to collaborate with Spike in writing some of The Goon Shows. Indeed, one of Spike's earliest writing partners, Larry Stephens, had accompanied him on that first hospital visit.

'Larry Stephens was a lovely man. He had been an officer in the army and served in India and he was also a brilliant jazz pianist, but he was a very quiet man. I don't think I ever heard him say more than about two words at one time and if you said something to him he would just blush.

'He was the sort of person that, when you walked into a room, you would miss him as you admired the wallpaper.'

While Spike and his co-writers put the words into the Goons' mouths, the performance skills of Peter Sellers made the characters come alive and gave

Curry and Chips was set in a factory manufacturing novelties.

them an enduring appeal.

'Peter Sellers created most of those characters and The Goon Show relied to a great extent on its characters. Once the characters were established, it was easy to write for them. They practically said the same things every week with catchphrases like 'Ooooh, he's fallen in the water' or 'You rotten swine!'. You always knew that when a big bomb had fallen on Bluebottle and blown him to smithereens there would be a pause and then he would say, 'You rotten swine!'.

'But in all young people, especially those interested in comedy, there is a sense of anarchy and The Goon Show was the first programme to be broadcast to the whole nation which presented scenes of seemingly uncontrolled anarchy. Every young person who grew up with the intention of being a writer or a comic actor adored The Goon Show. It was also a lot cleverer than it looked and there was a real freshness about the show.

'We had no such thing as canned laughter in those days and when the laughter is real you know that the show is working for the audience. That audience, of course, is representative of the rest of the country. There really was a bit of a comedy desert at that time with just small patches of greenery and The Goon Show was a flower in one of those patches. It started off a train of events that ran through each new generation of youngsters. It inspired Monty Python and even the Goodies, although that was never as good as Monty Python. Nevertheless, the influence of The Goon Show was there.'

Eric not only collaborated with Spike on the regular Goon Shows, but also on Archie In Goonland, which brought together The Goon Show and Educating Archie. He is a little vague about exactly whose idea this was.

'If you enjoyed it, it was my idea and if you didn't, it was Spike's!'

Eric's most enjoyable sequence from The Goon Show goes back to the morning which he and Spike spent in fits of laughter.

'That little bit where Spike and I were roaring with laughter at Major

Bloodnok is probably my favourite. A police inspector comes to visit him and Bloodnok come into the room and says, 'I had nothing to do with it. Whatever it was I had nothing to do with it. I never set foot on the mess funds!'.

'The inspector then says, 'No, no, it's a bequest. You have been left £10,000'

'Ah . . . yes, you want my brother.'

'You have a brother?'

'Yes, he's an identical twin. Excuse me.'

Then he leaves the room with a door-knob sound effect and the door opening and closing. Then there's the door knob again and the door opening and closing as he comes back in and says, 'My brother Dennis tells me you want to see me.'

'Yes, you've been bequeathed £10,000.'

'Ah, yes, I always thought I would be. I shall, naturally, give my twin brother Dennis some of it.'

'I didn't know you had a twin brother.'

'Oh, didn't you. Excuse me, I'll just introduce you.'

Then he leaves the room with the door knob and door opening and closing which is immediately repeated as he comes back in again.

'Yes, I'm Dennis. Did you want to see me about something? My brother said . . .' But the policeman is getting suspicious and says he wants to see them both together.

'No, we can never seen together. It's the curse of the Bloodnoks.'

'I don't understand.'

'We must never be in the same room together. I cannot explain it.'

'I insist, before handing over this money, on seeing you both together.'

'So be it!'

The door opens and closes, then opens and closes again.

'Here we are!'

'But there's only one of you.'

'There you are! The curse of the Bloodnoks has struck again!'

'All the going out and coming in, each time with a new excuse had us in fits of laughter. We could have kept him coming in and out of that door for twenty minutes, we were laughing so much at the cheek of the man.'

Spike once said of Eric that he was 'a little piece of gold in showbusiness' and they have been friends now for nearly fifty years, despite the fact that Spike does not play golf . . .

'I think it's probably because of the fact that he doesn't play golf that our friendship has lasted. I suppose I was quite well established when he wrote his first Crazy People and he must have respected what I had to say. That gives me a tremendous kick because Spike Milligan then continued writing in his own style. He created a style which has often been copied but never surpassed.'

Since The Goon Show ended, Spike has achieved great success on television, on stage, as a poet and as an author but Eric agrees with Harry Secombe that Spike, along with Harry and Peter Sellers, will be remembered first and foremost for the Goons.

'You can't say that Spike will be remembered for his books and poetry and stage appearances and The Goon Show and the television shows. It's too much. You can't be associated with all that at once and what does it matter, really?

'As long as there's something with your mark on it then you know your time on this earth has not been wasted. For Spike, it's The Goon Show.'

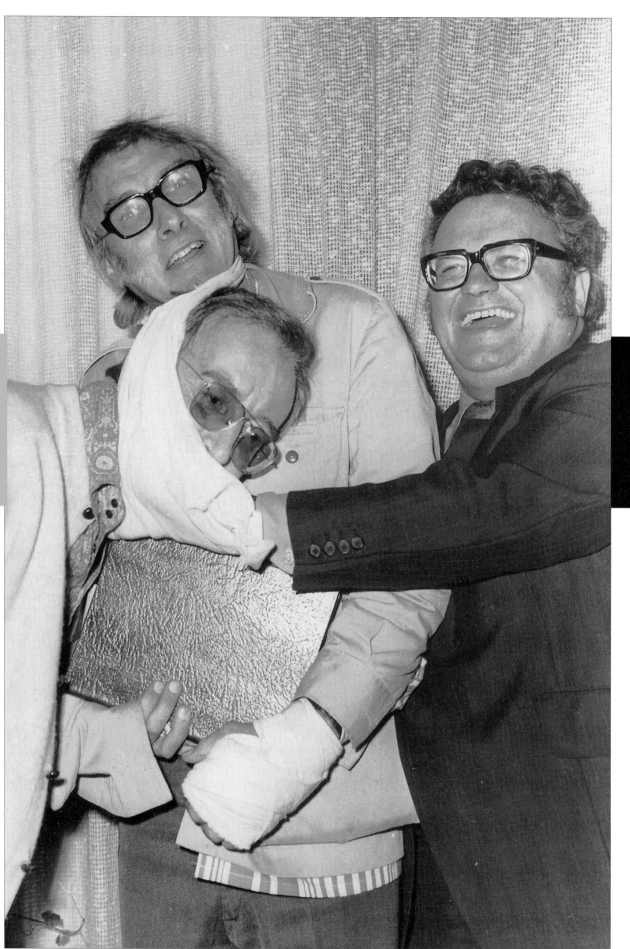

THE GOONS – The Story part 3

Despite Wallace Greenslade's pronouncement on the last radio Goon Show, the world had not seen the last of The Goon Shows. Getting out while they 'were still right on top' almost guaranteed strong, fond memories of the Shows and the characters. There would only be one more original Goon Show performed but through the 1960s such was the strength of 'folk memory' for the Goons and The Goon Show, aided by repeat broadcasts, that it was difficult for the performers to escape the 'Goon' label. Harry continued to be in demand as a singer/entertainer and sustained various forms of the TV show Secombe and Friends through the 1960s. Spike renewed his assault on TV comedy with his programme Spike Milligan Presents a Series of Unrelated Incidents at Current Market Value for BBC TV (thereby also declaring war on the typesetters of the Radio Times, one suspects), where some of the ideas aired for the Fred TV shows were explored a bit further. His success in the West End with the play Oblomov and Son of Oblomov lurked just around the corner. Peter began to discover one bitter lesson of growing film stardom: that celebrity attracts sycophants and hangers-on, and began to look back on The Goon Show days with that fondness and nostalgia that would haunt him for the rest of his life.

Hardly had the last Goon Show been transmitted, however, than the quintessential Goon 'short' The Running Jumping Standing Still Film became released on the cinema circuit in 1960. Only eleven minutes in length, it was originally filmed on a 16mm Piabolex camera that was Peter's latest toy in

Peter Sellers, aided by Harry Secombe, gets his head in Spike Milligan's sling.

Clowning in rehearsals with a hunchbacked Spike Milligan.

1959. Just about anyone and everyone who was available and had been associated with the Goons in the 1950s was involved. Each short gag sequence was filmed whenever they could afford to buy more film and during the last few Goon Shows Spike and Peter in particular would try out ideas. The long-suffering producer John Browell ruefully noted that 'very often they were rehearsing ideas for that film while we were trying to rehearse in the Camden Theatre, and sometimes I was not quite sure what performance I was rehearsing for.'

The producer of the TV Fred programmes, Dick Lester, was involved at the editing stages once the eleven-minute film had been completed. 'There was never any attempt during the filming of it, or during the post production of it, for it to be of any commercial use at all,' Dick recalled. "It was really just a chance to play around with his camera… it suddenly became a serious piece of filming. It started being shown in cinemas [from 35mm prints], and it opened in a news theatre near Piccadilly as Peter Sellers' Running Jumping Standing Still Film and then, when I had made Hard Day's Night, which was showing at the London Pavilion across from it, they changed it and it came back as Richard Lester's Running Jumping Standing Still Film and then Spike made a huge success with Son of Oblomov, or something, in the theatre that was down on Shaftesbury Avenue, and it became Spike Milligan's Running Jumping and Standing Still Film…!"

The film was nominated for an Academy Award and praised widely. Goonery had finally struck gold on film. It was viewed by at least one of the Beatles, since John Lennon (whom Lester directed in A Hard Days Night and Help!) went on to praise it as 'a rare and beautiful film… a masterpiece.'

The next manifestation of this Goon memory (albeit less successful) was the proposal in 1963 to reinvent The Goon Show characters in puppet form as The Telegoons. Since even the Goons themselves, when thinking about visualising the likes of Bluebottle or Eccles in the 1950s, had been going in the direction of some kind of animation, this idea was received positively. The proposal was to involve rod-and-string puppetry and documentary footage as necessary, to try and realise some of the crazier flights of Goon logic.

The project received firm and sustained attention. The original scripts, designed for live half-hour (-ish) performance, had to be adapted to the fifteen-minute length required by the animators. This task was undertaken by Maurice Wiltshire, who remained quite faithful to the flavour of the originals and had in fact collaborated on a couple of Goon Shows with Larry Stephens to produce pastiche Milligan when the writing pressure had been too much for Spike. The Variety format of musical interludes was redundant and a refocusing of the main comedy element meant that the original plot ideas of each script could be encapsulated for each Telegoon episode without much loss. Greenslade's part was either eliminated or passed over to Grytpype Thynne or Moriarty (who functioned as pseudo announcers as required by the plot).

One nice point about The Telegoons films was that small touches of visual humour were attempted from time to time, which might have been hinted at in the radio versions ('let them try that on television'). Jokes were made from the kinds of documentary footage used and also more subtle statements in the way that The Telegoons sets were made up – sometimes quite adult-type pictures and slogans would be lurking on the walls that would have meant noth-

The Goons with their puppets, the Telegoons.

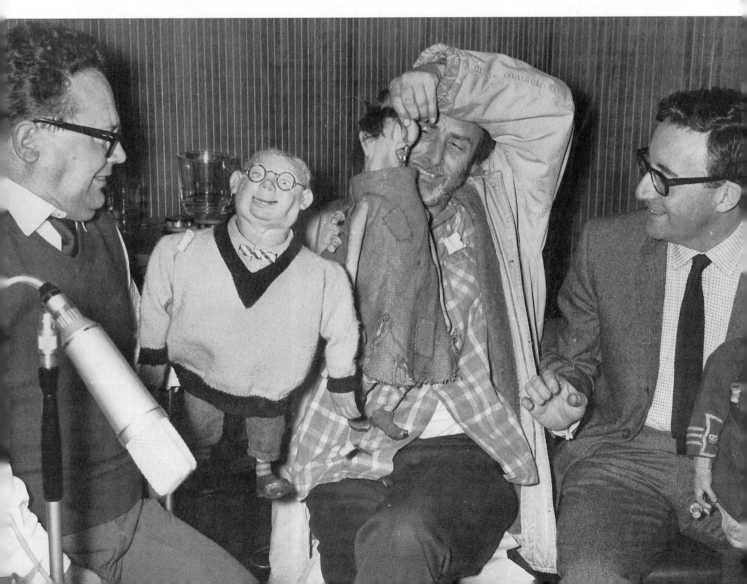

The Telegoon puppets were advertised as family viewing, not just for children.

ing at all to children watching just to see the puppets. The BBC must have been aware of this aspect, too, since The Telegoons were not advertised as a "kiddies-only" programme in the Radio Times but family viewing, preceding as they often did the more dramatic entertainment of Doctor Who in 1963 and 1964.

Ultimately, however, The Telegoons did not quite work as effectively as was wished. Everyone had their own idea of what the central Goon characters

looked like from the pictures behind their own eyes, to borrow Milligan's phrase. The actual puppets could not therefore satisfy everyone. The puppeteers worked hard with string puppet versions of the characters and the full-framed puppets for close up dialogue – work not helped by the fact that the Goons, characteristically, made life hard by ad-libbing when re-recording the sound tracks so the puppeteers' shooting scripts did not match up with the recordings!

Some of the scenes employing model sets could not hide the fact that normal size toys were being used to save money, which ruined the effect. When the Telegoon puppets re-enacted Napoleon's Piano it is very hard indeed to suspend any disbelief at the sight of puppets heaped on a piano, being rolled down a real street since the string puppets are obviously under little control (except in close-up, which for that scene they were not). Despite much effort to contain technical limitations over a filming programme which still produced 26 complete Telegoons episodes, the puppets did not make the hoped-for impact. Spike was so disappointed with the reception of the Telegoons that he has consistently refused to endorse any of the other projects that have since tried to bring the Goons to the screen in animated or puppet form.

Two other occasions during the 1960s brought the Goons back together in some guise of recreating the atmosphere of The Goon Show. The first of these was prompted by Harry in 1966, in the sense that the suggestion was made that a Goon Show script should be recreated and filmed to be included in part of an episode of Secombe and Friends for Associated Rediffusion TV.

The Goon Show finally chosen was 'The Whistling Spy Enigma' from 1955, all about conspiracies and exploding Hungarian football boots. The atmosphere created during the performance was quite Goonish and 'live' – a certain amount of clowning around at Harry's expense, since they were 'The Goons doing this for Harry Secombe's TV show.' Ray Ellington was also present and in good musical form. Spike in particular is delightfully unruly and nonconformist and this works well just as a performance. It is also further understandable when one realises that some production friction had occurred between Spike and the producer and some of his on-stage antics reflected this. Although the entire performance was filmed and still exists, only excerpts were ever shown in 1966 for Harry's show, or since.

The second project also suffered from some production problems. It again involved Peter Eton, now an independent film producer. On two or three occasions he did try to get the Goons together for projects, both then in 1968, and

much later in the mid 1970s, but his first effort made the most progress and Eton himself ruefully had to admit that 'it wasn't very successful'. He had been trying to persuade people for a long time (he had been saying it during his original tenure as producer) that the Goons were just as funny reading the scripts on TV as they were on radio but BBC sources were uninterested.

'I persuaded Thames to do it and the idea was just to have them reading their scripts with a great big Union Jack behind them... Then Spike locked himself in his room, refused to talk to me or talk to Norma his secretary, and he passed notices under the door saying 'I'm feeling ill, I can't write a thing' and this went on until

The Telegoons suffered from technical and budgetary limitations.

the actual day of the recording. This was a Sunday, and on the Saturday night he was still passing notes under the door, so I had to go down to the library and get an old Goon Show... Tales of Men's Shirts, we did."

The film print was specially preserved as it was the only example in existence of a filming process called Gemini, where video camera and 16mm film camera were strapped side by side during the shoot. It was also the first example of the Goons in action in colour. Even so, such con-

Prince Charles remains a huge fan of the Goons.

Below right: The screen behind Spike in this photograph is plain. Spike wrote on the photograph, 'An Attempt by Thames TV To Televise the Goon Show. The Show was Vetoed by Peter. I never knew why – was it because Harry and I were as funny as him?'

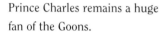

siderations could not hide a young John Cleese (as announcer) from looking progressively lost in the Goon chaos whilst the Goons enjoyed jokes together in front of the cameras. To cap it all, the programme had to be transmitted during a technicians' strike and therefore did not have the intended opening and closing credits which would otherwise have been provided.

1972 and the celebrations connected with the BBC's fiftieth anniversary of incorporation provided the backdrop for what was the final commissioned scripted performance of the Goons. It was intended to be a complimentary recognition by the BBC of how successful The Goon Show had been in firmly establishing a genre of radio comedy under the BBC banner. Peter and Harry were enthusiastic about the project and keen to take part. Great effort was put into contacting the other stalwart musicians who helped create and sustain the original Goon Show experience – Max Geldray, Ray Ellington, Andrew Timothy as announcer (Greenslade, sadly, had died in 1961). Wally Stott, maestro of the BBC orchestra-cum-band who originally underscored virtually all the Show's music, proved not to be available (as he was turning into Angela Morley).

Spike, however, had mixed feelings about a newly commissioned Last Goon Show of All for this event. It was not like previous occasions in the 1960s where already existing material had been re-used. John Browell was put in charge of production for the event. This Last Goon Show was already being talked about with anticipation after the official announcement, not the least because of the attendance of royalty at the event (Princess Anne, Prince Philip, Princess Margaret and Lord Snowdon). The production stakes were

An Attempt by Thomas TV. To release his
Cream Show. The Show was Vetoed by
Peter. I never knew why — was it
because Harry & I were as funny
as him?

MAY 1968

Christine Pryor played the girl
in Thame TV's Goon Show.

immediately much higher.

Perhaps unsurprisingly, therefore, Browell had an experience similar to
Peter Eton's in 1968 of getting material out of Spike. The creative process, after
all, is a lengthy one. Eventually, with about a week to go, the script reached
John on the Monday before recording (as in the days of the radio Shows).
Although very funny the script was deemed unsuitable.

This was mainly because of how the Royalty were written into the
script. Secombe was set to be the Queen – not just impersonate. Such
treatment in 1972 was utterly unacceptable to BBC production values and
code of practice (after all, many years were yet to pass before any such
ideas were made acceptable or vaguely palatable by the likes of Spitting
Image). Spike, of course, argued that the script should stay as it was. The
Goons were no strangers to controversy, after all. It was rather reminis-

cent of a Mexican stand-off.

The deabate raged almost right up to the day of the recording when Peter and Harry eventually persuaded Spike to work out a compromise. The three Goons sat down together during the first part of that day, working over a makeshift table in a secluded corner, making alterations which would take the controversial edges off Spike's script.

All of this put immense pressure on the technical side of the production since the time remaining to prepare sounds, effects, locate recordings became incredibly compressed. It was this aspect of the whole experience which probably accounts for Browell's reluctance to talk about the Show until fairly recently.

In the end, The Last Goon Show Of All got under way with a telegram, received and read out from an enraged Prince Charles, helplessly trapped in the

Top: Spike gives Ringo Starr a parking ticket.

Above: Spike and Peter at a party to mark Peter's decision to live in Ireland – for tax purposes.

Harry and Peter appeared together on Michael Parkinson's chat show.

Mediterranean on duty with HMS Norfolk:

'Last night my hair fell out and my knees dropped off with envy when I thought of my father and sister attending the show. Sometime, perhaps, you will find time to give a performance to a ship full of sea goons...'

The Goons performed one more time to a capacity, enthusiastic audience who greeted the reappearance of every familiar character with some affection. Secombe entered into the proceedings with characteristic Seagoon-ish zest; Sellers revelled in the opportunity to don once again the military trappings of Major Bloodnok and the suave voicings of Grytpype Thynne. Shared memories surfaced in the dialogue like 'Here is a preview of next winter in Jimmy Grafton's attic' (GRAMS: BLIZZARD), something easily recalled by Milligan the erstwhile 'prisoner of Zenda' in that selfsame attic after the war.

With some members of the Royal Family at The Last Goon Show of All.

Even so, The Last Goon Show of All is valuable more as a celebration of Goon nostalgia than for the comedy of the evening itself. It was not possible to flick a switch, as it were, and carry on as if this was just February 1960 and not an occasion twelve years after the radio shows ended. Harry remembers Peter and Spike first of all having some difficulty in rehearsal rediscovering the voices for Bluebottle and Eccles. It's perhaps not surprising, in view of the backstage altercations, that Spike himself seemed a little preoccupied during the Show, nor that at the end of the performance, he instructs the audience with wry seriousness, 'Now get out.'

Nevertheless, the evening had a live atmosphere and ended on a high note with much laughter, much playing to the press and a great deal of column space in papers the following day, from The Daily Express through to the august pages of The Times. Something that would have been hardly believable to a small group of demobbed entertainers meeting for a beer and a laugh and to share dreams at a small pub in London W1 in 1946.

The impact of The Goon Show lives on, although at this distance in time some of the echoes are slightly muted and muffled. Contemporary comedians of any standing acknowledge the influence of Milligan's ground breaking approach on their thinking and performance. The BBC's work in creative sound radio is still haunted by the achievements of The Goon Show with what one senior producer recently and appreciatively described as 'the final flowering of "stone age" technology.'

Whatever the technology that the Goons had had to rely on, combined with Milligan's imagination and the performing power of the Goons together, a comedy show emerged that has yet to find an equal in British post-war history.

A clip from Ghost in the Noonday Sun, starring Peter Sellers and six Spike Milligans.

MAX GELDRAY'S STORY

Dutch harmonica player Max Geldray contributed more than just music to The Goon Show. He was a very experienced and highly respected jazz musician and had been in the entertainment business longer than any of the regular Goons. As he says himself, 'I was the oldest then, and I'm still the oldest!'. Max maintains, of course, that music formed an integral part of The Goon Show.

'Music was vital to The Goon Shows. It helped to create an atmosphere. It was all real, nothing was an imitation on that show, and as a result I have all sorts of musicians coming to me to talk about the show. The Grateful Dead were great fans of the music and the show and Elton John, who has all the original scripts, told me how much he had been influenced by the music on The Goon Shows and how much he enjoyed it.'

Respect for Mr Geldray and the tremendous discipline exerted on such a seemingly indisciplined rabble, ensured that the Goonery never encroached on the show's musical interludes, but Milligan, Secombe and Sellers did enjoy being given the odd opportunity to join in.

'While I was playing there might sometimes be some mucking about behind me but usually they would literally be. "Round the back for the old brandeee!!". Harry would usually bring it with him, sometimes mixed with milk, which he said was good for the stomach!

'I don't know which shows they were, but I do remember Spike playing the introduction on guitar – I think that happened twice. The shows always

Max Geldray was an integral part of the show.

Max Geldray on stage in a strong man sketch with Sellers and Milligan.

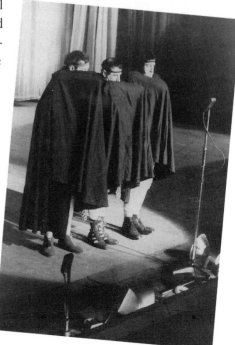

The show always ended with a musical interlude . . .

ended with me playing Crazy Rhythm. That way, when the show was cut they could always be sure it was the right length by letting Crazy Rhythm run on a little longer. Ray Ellington played the bongos on that, but when I did a Latin American number, all the boys would pick up a rhythm instrument of some kind and play along.'

Max became great friends with all of the Goons and, after he moved to live in America, he kept in touch, especially with Sellers who spent so much time in Hollywood and would visit Max whenever he could. But Max remembers the real Peter Sellers being hard to pin down.

'There was certainly a great rapport on the show and it was tremendous fun. I was very close to Peter. He used to call me up and ask me over to his house to play with his gadgets – new tape recorders, hi-fi and such. He was a good friend and good fun. He would come over to the States a lot. I don't think that he felt there was a real Peter Sellers. Sometimes he would just live the characters he played.'

It was always hard to suppress Peter's innate sense of fun, however, and Max would often find himself on the receiving end of some very strange phone calls.

'Peter used to call me Plooge because of The Goon Shows and the 'Fred' shows. They made me say "Ploogee!", you see, and I had to exaggerate my voice so that it was even higher. He would phone me up and use my voice. It was very strange talking to myself on the phone and he wouldn't let up for a long time. We would have entire conversations with him mimicking me.'

Sellers wasn't the only Goon to drop in on Max after he had made his home in the States. Michael Bentine was a regular visitor, too.

'I also knew Michael very well. He used to come over to Palm Springs for several months each year. He was very artistic with wonderful ideas. When he was with The Goon Show, he and Spike had so many ideas it was always difficult to know who thought of what. With so many creative people around there were bound to be clashes, but I never saw any major ones. I was never aware of any friction.

'I think Michael wanted to go out further in the world with his ideas. I can honestly say he was one of the nicest people I ever met – a really lovely man and we shared many laughs.'

While Max remained firm friends with Michael after his departure from the Goons, his admiration for Spike grew as the Goons surged on from strength to strength.

'As a result of Spike's writing, the humour in Britain changed. That is a great achievement and the effects are still being felt today. Spike made sure that everything on that show was superior including, of course, the sound effects. These were the best around, at the insistence of Spike. He never had secondhand ones, they were all marvellous sounds. The antics of the sound men used to get a great laugh from the audience as they watched them going up and down stairs or open and close doors. The audience used to love it.'

. . . and Sellers and Milligan would sometimes play along.

Max performed with the Goons, or rather Sellers and Milligan, on stage but also went on to take part in A Show Called Fred and the Son Of Fred shows.

'There was one particularly funny incident that I recall from one of the Fred shows. I did my number, and as I did I walked out of the studio. I was immaculately dressed in a mohair suit and I came to the front of the studio still playing (of course there was a backing track and I was miming) and being followed by the cameras. Still walking, I put my thumb out for a lift and a car stopped. The audience didn't know but the driver was Dick Lester, the director. I got into the car and we drove off. I was still playing and the driver got fed up and threw me out. I was in the middle of the countryside.

Geldray was more than just a great harmonica player.

'I started walking again, still playing, and I came to some water. I took off my shoes and socks and rolled up my trousers. I went through the water, still playing and came up on the other side. I was now on a thoroughfare with my shoes and socks in one hand, my trousers rolled up and I was playing the harmonica. The road was the main road to Scotland and there were all these truck drivers going past. We had a theory that they would never tell anyone about it because who would believe them? Would you tell? People would think you were crazy! That was visual Goon humour.'

Contrary to what some of his contemporaries recall, Max remembers there being quite a few unscheduled departures from the script during The Goon Show recordings, although he is doubtful about how much of it survived to be broadcast. One thing, however, over which the BBC had no control was its artistes' dress sense . . .

'There was a lot of ad-libbing in The Goon Show. Some had to be cut out, not only because it was a bit dubious, but because it went on for too long. I remember once as well, when Peter was learning judo, he came and did the entire show in his judo outfit.

'The shows were such fun. I have many happy memories. I enjoyed it all so much.'

BLUEBOTTLE'S STORY

Without doubt one of the best-loved of the Goons characters, Bluebottle was the target for much of the Goonery broadcast on air. A victim he may have been, but with good reason. The character of Bluebottle was based on one of the Goons' real-life victims, a certain Ruxton Hayward . . .

Ruxton Hayward, upon whom the character of Bluebottle was based.

'When I left school I was still attached to my school Scout troop. One year they decided they should have a celebrity to open their fete and they asked me if I could try to contact John Gregson or Gordon Jackson. Unfortunately, they were heavily guarded by the Rank "charm school" and I never got past the secretary. Next they suggested that I approach the new comic outfit, the Goons. I really liked them and I trotted off to the Chiswick Empire to confront Michael Bentine . . .'

Ruxton, it must be said, has a rather distinctive voice remarkably similar to that of Bluebottle. He would also admit to being something of an eccentric and Bentine's reaction to meeting Ruxton was . . . understandable.

'Michael very kindly received me, heard me out and told me that I ought to see the rest of the boys. He said I was a genius and sent me with that very message to meet the others at the Shepherd's Bush Empire.

'So there I was at the Shepherd's Bush Empire telling Peter, Harry and Spike that Michael Bentine had sent me and I was to tell them that he said I was a genius. Well, they were all ears! Peter said, "Of course you are, my boy!". Unknown to me, "genius" was their code for "Here's a right mug!". I was being given the bum's rush but naively believing that I was making an impression –

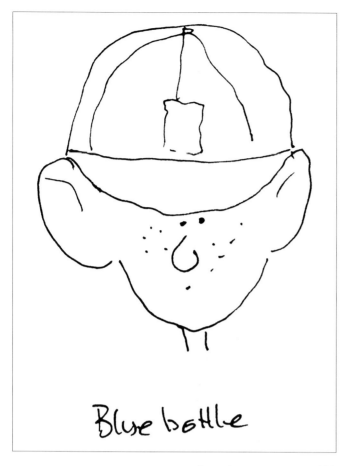

Blue bottle

but wasn't I, though, dressed in my short trousers and uniform jacket!'.

The Goons would later freely admit that the character of Bluebottle had been based on Ruxton, but the story doesn't end there. Hardly the shy and retiring type, Ruxton took to the stage himself, intent on pursuing a showbiz career, and was almost drafted into the Honourable Company of Goons as an extra . . .

'Some time later, I was in Luton, having finished a summer season, and the Goons told Mr Sherman, the owner of the theatre in which I had appeared, that they needed a comic stooge for one of their gags. He said, "I've the very person for you" and called me over, whence I came, prancing across with my usual "Have I come to the right place?". Then I was confronted with the boys!

'I could see them eyeing each other, looking me up and down and all thinking, "Here's a right mug!" Then Peter Sellers started chatting to me:

'Now, dear boy' He spoke like that. 'Now, dear boy, we were looking for a comedian in our show and we were wondering if you could play the part, but of course you would have to wear short trousers . . .'

'I am wearing short trousers!'

'Why, so you are, dear boy, but you would have to have a beard . . .'

'I do have a beard!'

'So you have, dear boy, but you would have to wear glasses . . .'

'I am wearing glasses!'

'This went on until he had described me down to a 'T'. Then he said, 'Do you know, dear boy, I do think you could be our comedian.' To which I replied, 'What's a comedian?'. Sellers said, 'Oh, he makes people laugh.' I said, 'Sorry' and walked away! When they later came to broadcast The Goon Show they didn't really need me: they had Peter Sellers to impersonate me!'

Despite his two encounters with the fledgling Goons, Ruxton didn't actually twig that Bluebottle was him until he again heard himself being described 'to a 'T'' by Peter Sellers, this time on TV.

'I didn't realise that Bluebottle was based on me until Peter Sellers said so on Parkinson Meets The Goons in 1972. It was just natural behaviour to me. I do know that people have always liked to impersonate my voice, and apparently I am instantly recognisable. I wonder if other people ever suspected that Bluebottle was based on me? It is always the victim who is the last to know . . . but I feel privileged to have influenced the Goons.

'I have developed other acts Bluebottle-style, such as Bearded Schoolboy, Happy Sandboy and Wooly Wolfcub. I suppose I do have a private life and a public life but I wouldn't like to say where they separate or where they overlap – I'm still Ruxton!

'I remember at one Goons Preservation Society get-together recently, Harry Secombe was the guest celebrity and, though he waved politely at me, I'm sure that all day long he was desperately trying to remember why he knew me!'

THE GOON SHOWS

First Series

Billed as: 'CRAZY PEOPLE, featuring Radio's own Crazy Gang – "The Goons".'

Cast: Peter Sellers, Harry Secombe, Spike Milligan, Michael Bentine, The Ray Ellington Quartet, The Stargazers, Max Geldray, and (except where stated) the BBC Dance Orchestra, conducted by Stanley Black. Announcer Andrew Timothy, except nos. 8-10, announcer Denys Drower.

Scripts written by Spike Milligan and Larry Stephens, edited by Jimmy Grafton. Produced by Dennis Main Wilson, except 11-14, produced by Leslie Bridgmont. Nos. 1-9 broadcast on Mondays, nos. 10-17 on Thursdays. All pre-recorded the previous Sunday.

The shows consist of four or five short sketches separated by musical items.

1	28/5/51	9	23/7/51
2	4/6/51	10	2/8/51
3	11/6/51	11	9/8/51
4	18/6/51	12	16/8/51
5	25/65/1	13	23/8/51
6	2/7/51	14	30/8/51
7	9/7/51	15	6/9/51
8	16/7/51	16	13/9/51
		17	20/9/51

SP   26/12/51
CINDERELLA (pantomime)
with Lizbeth Webb as Cinderella, Graham Stark as Prince Charming: The Goons: The Stargazers: The Ray Ellington Quartet: Max Geldray and the Augmented Dance Orchestra conducted by Stanley Black. Produced by Dennis Main Wilson. Recorded 16/12/51

Second Series

Billed as 'The Goon Show, featuring these crazy people. . .'

Cast and musicians as for the previous series for the first six shows, after which the Stargazers left.

Spike Milligan and Larry Stephens, edited by Jimmy Grafton (who also wrote special lyrics for some shows).

Produced by Dennis Main Wilson. Broadcast Tuesdays, pre-recorded the previous Sunday (except nos. 24 and 25).

1	22/1/52	13	22/4/52
2	29/1/52	14	29/4/52
3	5/2/52	15	6/5/52
	12/2/52	16	13/5/52
No transmission owing to the		17	20/5/52
death of King George 6th		18	27/5/52
4	19/2/52	19	3/6/52
(BBC Dance Orch. cond. by		(with the BBC Revue Orch.	
Stanley Andrews)		cond. by Robert Busby)	
5	26/2/52	20	10/6/52
6	4/3/52	(with the BBC Revue Orch.	
7	11/3/52	cond. by Wally Stott)	
8	18/3/52	21	17/6/52
The Goons' version of Rider		(without Bentine)	
Haggard's 'She' entitled 'Her'		22	24/6/52
9	25/3/52	23	1/7/52
10	1/4/52	24	8/7/52
11	8/4/52	(recorded 29/6/52)	
(without Milligan)		25	15/7/52
12	15/4/52	(recorded 6/7/52)	

Third Series

From now on billed as 'THE GOON SHOW'.

Basic cast: Sellers, Secombe, Milligan, with Geldray, Ellington and orchestra conducted by Wally Stott. Announcer Andrew Timothy. Bentine has now left.

Produced by Peter Eton, except 18 & 19 produced by Charles Chilton.

Scripts by Spike Milligan and Larry Stephens, edited by Jimmy Grafton.

All except 7 broadcast Tuesdays: pre-recorded the previous Sunday (except 20-22).

The shows have three parts; the title given is usually that of the middle episode.

1	11/11/52	Fred of the Islands
2	18/11/52	The Egg of the Great Auk
3	25/11/52	I Was a Male Fan Dancer
4	2/12/52	The Saga of HMS Aldgate
5	9/12/52	The Expedition for Toothpaste
6	16/12/52	The Archers (without Milligan)
7	26/12/52	Robin Hood (Christmas Pantomime – 45 mins: without Milligan; with Dick Emery & Carole Carr)
8	30/12/52	Where does Santa Claus Go in the Summer? (without Milligan; with Ellis Powell)
9	6/1/53	The Navy, Army, and Air Force (without Millgan, with Dick Emery)
10	13/1/53	The British Way of Life (without Milligan, with Graham Stark)
11	20/1/53	A Survey of Britain (without Milligan, with Dick Emery)
12	27/1/53	Flint of the Flying Squad (without Milligan, with Graham Stark)
13	3/2/53	Seaside Resorts in Winter (without Milligan, with Dick Emery)
14	10/2/53	The Tragedy of Oxley Towers (without Milligan, with Graham Stark & Valentine Dyall)
15	17/2/53	The Story of Civilization (without Milligan, with Dick Emery)
16	24/2/53	The Search for the Bearded Vulture (without Milligan, with Graham Stark)
17	3/3/53	The Mystery of the Monkey's Paw (with out Milligan, with Dick Emery)
18	10/3/53	The Mystery of the Cow on the Hill
19	17/3/53	Where Do Socks Come From?
	24/3/53	No transmission owing to the death of Queen Mary
20	31/3/53	The Man Who Never Was (recorded 22/3/53)
21	7/4/53	The Building of the Suez Canal (recorded 29/3/53)
22	14/4/53	The De Goonlies (recorded 5/4/53)
23	21/4/53	The Conquest of Space
23	28/4/53	The Ascent of Mount Everest
25	5/5/53	The Story of Plymouth Hoe Armarda
SP	3/6/53	Coronation edition (40 mins; recorded 1/6/53; without Geldray; with Graham Stark)

Fourth Series

Scripts 1-9 and 11-20 by Spike Milligan and Larry Stephens; no. 10 by Larry Stephens; remainder by Spike Milligan.

Announcer Andrew Timothy (nos.1-5); then Wallace Greenslade.

Produced by Peter Elton, except no. 15 produced by Jacques Brown.

Nos. 1-20 (except 13, broadcast on Fridays, nos. 21-30 on Mondays; all pre-recorded the previous Sunday.

1	2-10/53	The Dreaded Piano Clubber
2	9/10/53	The Man Who Tried to Destroy London's Monuments
3	16/10/53	The Ghastly Experiments of Dr. Hans Eidelburger
4	23/10/53	The Building of Britain's First Atomic Cannon
5	30/10/53	The Gibraltar Story
6	6/11/53	Through the Sound Barrier in an Airing Cupboard
7	13/11/53	TheFirst Albert Memorial to the Moon
8	20/11/53	The Missing Beaurocrat
9	27/11/53	Operation Bagpipes
10	4/12/53	The Flying Saucer Mystery
11	11/12/53	The Spanish Armarda
12	18/12/53	The British Way
SP	25/12/53	Short insert in 'Christmas Crackers' (which also contained contributions from other Variety shows) (recorded 20/12/53)
13	26/12/53	The Giant Bombardon (with Michael Bentine)
14	1/1/54	Ten Thousand Fathoms Down in a Wardrobe
15	8/1/54	The Missing Prime Minister
16	15/1/54	Dr. Jekyll and Mr. Crun
17	22/1/54	The Mummified Priest
18	29/1/54	The History of Communications
19	5/2/54	The Kippered Herring Gang
20	12/2/54	The Toothpaste Expedition
21	15/2/54	The Case of the Vanishing Room
22	22/2/54	The Great Ink Drought of 1902
23	1/3/54	The Greatest Mountain in the World
24	8/3/54	The Collapse of the British Railway Sandwich System
25	15/3/54	The Silent Bugler
26	22/3/54	Western Story
27	29/3/54	The Saga of the Internal Mountain
28	5/4/54	The Invisable Acrobat (Ellington pre-recorded)
29	12/4/54	The Great Bank of England Robbery (Ellington pre-recorded)
30	19/4/54	The Siege of Fort Knight (Ellington pre-recorded)
SP	11/6/54	ARCHIE IN GOON LAND with Peter Brough and Archie Andrews, Peter Sellers, Spike Milligan, Harry Secombe, Hatti Jacques and the BBC Variety Orchestra, conductor Paul Fenoulhet. Script by Eric Sykes and Spike Milligan. Produced by Roy Speer. Recorded 6/5/54
SP	1/ 8/54	THE STARLINGS Peter Sellers, Harry Secombe, Spike Milligan and Andrew Timothy. Written by Spike Milligan. Without musicians or audience. Produced by Peter Eton. Recorded 11 / 12/8/54

Fifth Series

From now on the announcer is Wallace Greenslade. Scripts for shows 1-6 by Spike Milligan, remainder by Milligan and Eric Sykes. Produced by Peter Eton. Broadcast Tuesdays, pre-recorded the previous Sunday, except nos. 14 and 20.

1	28/ 9/54	The Whistling Spy Enigma
2	5/10/54	The Lost Gold Mine (of Charlotte)
3	12/10/54	The Dreaded Batter-Pudding Hurler (of Bexhill-on-Sea)
4	19/10/54	The Phantom Head Shaver (of Brighton)
5	26/10/54	The Affair of the Lone Banana
6	2/11/54	The Canal (with Valentine Dyall)
7	9/11/54	Lurgi Strikes Britain (TS: Lurgi Strikes Again)
8	16/11/54	The Mystery of the Marie Celeste (Solved)
9	23/11/54	The Last Tram (from Clapham)
10	0/11/54	The Booted Gorilla (found?)
11	7/12/54	The Spanish Suitcase
12	14/12/54	Dishonoured, or The Fall of Neddie Seagoon
13	21/12/54	Forog
14	28/12/54	Ye Bandit of Sherwood Forest (recorded 19/12/54: with Charlotte Mitchell)
15	4/1/55	Nineteen-Eighty-Five (orch. cond. by Bruce Campbell)
16	11/I/55	The Case of the Missing Heir
17	18/1/55	China Story
18	25/1/55	Under Two Floorboards–A Story of the Legion
19	1/ 2/55	The Missing Scroll
20	8/ 2/55	Nineteen/Eighty/Five (recorded 30/1/55: with John Snagge–pre-rec.)
21	15/2/55	The Sinking of Westminster Pier
22	22/2/55	The Freball of Milton Street
23	1/3/55	The Six Ingots of Leadenhall Street
24	8/2/55	Yehti
25	15/3/55	The White Box of Great Bardfield
26	22/3/55	The End (TS:—reissue only: Confessions of a Secret Senna-pod Drinker

Sixth Series

Scripts by Spike Milligan (SM) except where indicated; (ES) Eric Sykes, (LS) Larry Stephens. Produced by Peter Eton (nos. 1-21) and Pat Dixon (nos. 22-27). Broadcast Tuesdays, pre-recorded the previous Sunday (except nos.10 & 15).

1	20/ 9/55	The Man Who Won the War (SM & ES) (TS:Seagoon MCC)
2	27/ 9/55	The Secret Escritoire (SM & ES)
3	4/10/55	The Lost Emperor
4	11/10/55	Napoleon's Piano
5	18/10/55	The Case of the Missing CD Plates
6	25/10/55	Rommel's Treasures
7	1/11 55	Foiled by President Fred
8	8/11/55	Shangri-La Again
9	15/11/55	The International Christmas Puddings
	22/11/55	(No.10 postponed to ~/4/56,3 replaced by repeat of 'China Story', first broadcast 18/1/55)
11	29/11/55	The Sale of Manhattan (TS: The Lost Colony)
12	6/12/55	The Terrible Revenge of Fred Fu-Manchu

SP 8/12/55 The Missing Christmas Parcel–Post Early for Christmas (ES) (15 minutes–broadcast in Children's Hour; recorded 27/11/55: without musicians). Devised and produced by Peter Eton and John Lane

13	13/12/55	The Lost Year
14	20/12/55	The Greenslade Story (with John Snagge)
15	27/12/55	The Hastings Flyer–Robbed (recorded 18/12/55)
16	3/ 1/56	The Mighty Wurlitzer
17	10/ 1/56	The Raid of the International Christmas Pudding
18	17/ 1/56	Tales of Montmartre (SM & ES) (with Charlotte Mitchell)
19	24/ 1/56	TheJet-Propelled Guided NAAFI
20	31/ 1/56	The House of Teeth (with Valentine Dyall)
21	7/ 2/56	Tales of Old Dartmoor (orch. cond. by Bruce Campbell)
22	14/ 2/56	The Choking Horror (orch. cond. by Bruce Campbell)
23	21/ 2/56	The Great Tuscan Salami Scandal (without musicians, with John Snagge pre-rec.)
24	28/ 2/56	The Treasure in the Lake (orch. cond. Bruce Campbell)

SP 1/ 3/56 The Goons Hit Wales (51-2 minute insert in St. David's Day programme, recorded 26/2/56)

25	6/3/56	The Fear of Wages (SM & LS)
26	13/ 3/56	Scradje (SM & LS) (with John Snagge–pre-rec.)
27	20/ 3/56	The Man Who Never Was (SM & LS)
10	3/ 4/56	The Pevensey Bay Disaster (recorded 20/11 /55)

SP 29/ 8/56 China Story (SM & ES)I7 (recorded 24/8/56 at the National Radio Show. Produced by Dennis Main Wilson)

Seventh Series

Scripts by Milligan and Larry Stephens, except nos. 2 and 23, by Milligan only. Produced by Pat Dixon, except nos. 1 and 2 produced by Peter Eton. Broadcast Thursdays, except nos. 10 and 13 broadcast Wednesdays. Pre-recorded the previous Sunday (except nos. 6, 14, 15 and 16).

1	4/10/56	The Nasty Affair at the Burami Oasis
2	11/10/56	Drums Along the Mersey (with Valentine Dyall)
3	18/10/56	The Nadger Plague
4	25/10/56	The MacReekie Rising of '74 (without Milligan, with George Chisholm)
5	1/11/56	The Spectre of Tintagel (with Valentine Dyall) (no. 6 postponed to 14/2/57 replaced by repeat of 'The Greenslade Story', first broadcast 20/12/55)
7	15/11/56	The Great Bank Robbery
8	22/11/56	Personal Narrative
9	29/11/56	The Mystery of the Fake Neddie Seagoons (TS: The Case of The Fake Neddie Seagoons)
SP for TS only		Robin Hood (with Valentine Dyall and Dennis Price) (recorded 2/12/56; not broad cast in Britain)
10	5/12/56	What's My Line
11	13/12/56	The Telephone
12	20/12/56	The Flea
SP	24/12/56	GOS only Operation Christmas Duff (special overseas edition— recorded 9/12/56)
13	26/12/56	Six Charlies in Search of an Author
14	3/1/57	Emperor of the Universe (rec. 23/12/56
15	10/1/57	Wings Over Dagenham (rec. 30/12/56) (with George Chisholm)
16	17/1/57	The Rent Collectors (rec. 30/12/56) (with Bernard Miles)
17	24/1/57	Shifting Sands (with Jack Train)
18	31/1/57	The Moon Show
19	7/2/57	The Mysterious Punch-up-the-Conker
6	14/2/57	The Sleeping Prince (recorded 4/11/56)
20	21/2/57	Round the World in Eighty Days
21	28/2/57	Insurance, the White Man's Burden
22	7/3/57	The Africa Ship Canal
23	14/3/57	Ill Met by Goonlight
24	21/3/57	The Missing Boa Constrictor
25	28/3/57	The Histories of Pliny the Elder

Eighth Series

Scripts by Spike Milligan (SM), Larry Stephens (LS), John Antrobus JA), and Maurice Wiltshire (MW), as indicated. Produced by Charles Chilton (nos. 1-5 and 17-26), Roy Speer (nos. 6-14), and Tom Ronald (nos.15 and 16). Broadcast Mondays, pre-recorded the previous Sunday (except no. 18).

1	30/ 9/57	Spon (SM) (without Secombe, with Dick Emery)
2	7/10/57	The Junk Affair (SM & LS)

3	14/10/57	The Burning Embassy (SM & LS)
4	21/10/57	The Great Regent's Park Swim (SM & LS)
5	28/10/57	The Treasure in the Tower (SM & LS)
6	4/11/57	The Space Age (SM & LS)
7	11/11/57	The Red Fort (SM & LS)
8	18/11/57	The Missing Battleship (SM & LS) (without Geldray)
9	25/11/57	The Policy (SM & LS)
10	2/12/57	King Solomon's Mines (SM & LS)
11	9/12/57	The Stolen Postman (LS)
12	16/12/57	The Great British Revolution (SM & LS)
13	23/12/57	The Plasticine Man (SM & LS) (without Ellington)
14	30/12/57	African Incidentl (SM & LS) (with Cecile Chevreau)
15	6/1/58	The Thing on the Mountain (LS & MW)
16	13/1/58	The String Robberies (SM) (with George Chisholm)
17	20/1/58	The Moriarty Murder Mystery (LS & MW)
18	27/1/58	The Curse of Frankenstein (SM) (rec. 19/1/58)(without Ellington, with George Chisholm)
19	3/2/58	The White Neddie Trade (LS & MW)
20	10/2/58	Ten Snowballs that Shook the World (SM)
21	17/2/58	The Man Who Never Was (SM & LS)
22	24/2/58	World War One (SM) (TS: '_____!')
23	3/3/58	The Spon Plague (SM &JA) (with George Chisholm)
24	10/3/58	Tiddleywinks (SM) (with JohnSnagge)
25	17/3/58	The Evils of Bushey Spon (SM) (with A. E. Matthews)
26	24/3/58	The Great Statue Debate (SM &JA)

'Vintage Goons'

A series recorded specially for TS. Scripts by Spike Milligan. Produced by Charles Chilton (nos. 1, 2, & 9-14), Roy Speer (nos. 3-7), and Tom Ronald (no. 8) Recorded Sundays together with 8th series shows.

1	6/ 10/57	The Mummified Priest
2	20/10/57	The Greatest Mountain in the World
3	3/11/57	The Missing Ten Downing Street
4	17/11/57	The Giant Bombardon (with Valentine Dyall)
5	1/12/57	The Kippered Herring Gang
6	15/12/57	The Vanishing Room
7	29/12/57	The Ink Shortage
8	12/1/58	The Mustard and Cress Shortage
9	16/2/58	The Internal Mountain
10	23/2/58	The Silent Buglers
11	2/3/58	The Great Bank of England Robberys
12	9/3/58	The Dreaded Piano Clubber
13	16/3/58	The Siege of Fort Night
14	23/3/58	The Albert Memorial

Ninth Series

Scripts by Spike Milligan (except no. 7). Produced by John Browell. Broadcast Mondays, except no. 12 broadcast Tuesday; pre-recorded previous Sunday.

1	3/11/58	The Sahara Desert Statue
2	10/11/58	I Was Monty's Treble
3	17/11/58	The £ l,000,000 Penny
4	24/11/58	The Pam's Paper Insurance Policy
5	1/12/58	The Mountain Eaters
6	8/12/58	The Childe Harolde Rewarde
7	15/12/58	The Seagoon Memoirs (script by Larry Stephens and Maurice Wiltshire)
8	22/12/58	Queen Anne's Rain
9	29/12/58	The Battle of Spion Kop
10	5/1/59	Ned's Atomic Dustbin '(with John Snagge – pre-rec.)
11	12/1/59	Who Is Pink Oboe? (without Sellers; with Kenneth Connor, Valentine Dyall, Graham Stark, Jack Train and John Snagge, (who was pre-rec.)
12	20/1/59	The Call of the West
I3	26/1/59	Dishonoured – Again
14	2/2/59	The Scarlet Capsule (with Andrew Timothy – pre-rec.)
15	9/2/59	The Tay Bridge (with George Chisholm)
16	16/2/59	The Gold Plate Robbery
17	23/2/59	The £50 Cure (without Secombe, with Kenneth Connor)

Tenth Series

Scripts by Spike Milligan.Produed by John Browell. Broadcast Thursdays, pre-recorded the previous Sunday.

1	24/12/59	A Christmas Carol
2	31/12/59	The Tale of Men's Shirts
3	7/1/60	The Chinese Legs (with John Snagge – pre-rec.)
4	14/1/60	Robin's Post
5	21/1/60	The Silver Dubloons (with Valentine Dyall)
6	28/1/60	The Last Smoking Seagoon (with John Snagge – pre-rec.)